MIND MC

First published 1990

© JENNY RANDLES 1990

British Library Cataloguing in Publication data

Randles, Jenny
Mind monsters: invaders from inner space?
1. Monsters
I. Title
001.9'44

ISBN 0-85030-829-1

*The Aquarian Press is part of the Thorsons Publishing Group,
Wellingborough, Northamptonshire, NN8 2RQ, England*

Typeset by Harper Phototypesetters Limited, Northampton, England
Printed in Great Britain by Woolnough Bookbinding Limited,
Irthlingborough, Northamptonshire.

3 5 7 9 10 8 6 4 2

Acknowledgements

I am grateful to all the researchers mentioned in the text. I have tried to credit their invaluable work at source, but if I missed anybody out I apologize. *Fortean Times* cannot be recommended highly enough to anyone who enjoyed this book; and whilst I hate singling out any individual for special mention, I must do this to the following because they offered material above and beyond my expectations: Keith Basterfield in Australia, Don Worley in the USA, and in Britain, Michele Clare, Dave Clarke, Bill Gibbons, Michael Goss, Peter Hough, Clive Potter and Roy Sandbach.

Introduction: The Case
of the Ninja Dwarfs

I was amazed to see how many people have had experiences of
this kind and how carefully the secret was guarded.

Carl Jung, psychologist

Not very far from where I live is a strange house. It looms above
the River Mersey like some Gothic mansion, yet is curiously
trapped within the technological barriers of the twentieth
century.

Above its ruddy brick walls can be heard the scream of aircraft
engines as they trail like banshees across Cheadle, Cheshire,
heading towards the bustle of Manchester International Airport
three miles away. If you walk through the trees that fence in this
impressive building you will arrive unexpectedly at a place
where cars hurtle down a busy new motorway.

There could scarcely be a less likely setting in which to find
a monster. But if the tales that are emerging from the grounds
of Abney Hall are to be believed, this is precisely what you face
on a dark and dreadful night. However, perhaps the most
significant question of this and other monster stories is whether
the tales *are* to be believed.

My colleague Roy Sandbach introduced me to the case of
Cheadle's Ninja dwarfs. Through a mutual friend we met
Pauline,* a teenage girl who had been at the centre of the affair.
She had a very chilling story to relate.

* Indicates the name used is a pseudonym

In turn the various members of the group all developed stories to relate. One of the instructors claimed to have been attacked by 'it', feeling a force on his throat that was choking the breath out of him. He fought it off and collapsed into a heap. Then, according to other members of this intrepid band, he crawled off in the direction of the river and they had to pull him away, fearful that he would drown himself.

Even Pauline claims that this force took hold and made her attack her boyfriend (who was also with the group). It took four youngsters to drag the semi-maniacal girl away, such was the demonic power that seemed to possess her.

Another of the boys was allegedly thrown against a wall by an invisible force which they attribute to this thing. One of the girls fell asleep on a bench after class and woke up to see the dark form hovering in mid air directly above her. A hand then stretched out towards her paralysed form until, recovering composure, she ran from the place as fast as possible.

Pauline had no doubt that the entity was some sort of monster that fed on their energy. 'It preys on the bad part of everyone it comes into contact with,' she insisted.

By October they had all had enough. Even towards the last they had seen red and green eyes glowing in the bushes and heard a story from one of the night guards at the site that he had confronted some small figures in Ninja uniforms (some black and others green) which vanished as if they had melted into the night.

Now the would-be martial artists decided to move on and hold their sessions somewhere else. The prospect of cold winter nights in the grounds of Abney Hall, and having to share them with a thing of unknown origin, lost a great deal of its attraction.

In essence this was the story that Roy Sandbach and I discovered as we began to explore the monster on our doorsteps. We were used to investigating all sorts of peculiar cases, but this was something novel even for us.

The reaction of any sober-minded individual would probably be to regard this saga as a combination of fertile imaginations and mass hysteria. Yet Roy knew Pauline's family. It was not quite so simple to dismiss this affair out of hand.

Besides, here was a prime example of a latter-day monster in urban surroundings. It seemed almost inconceivable that one

could turn up in 1988 close to heavily populated areas and midway between the city of Manchester and the town of Stockport.
Yet that was the claim now set before us.

It was ripe for exploration and investigation to see if any clues
could be gleaned about the genesis of a monster legend. Perhaps
ghostly Ninja dwarfs were no different from the Loch Ness
Monster or grotesque aliens on kidnap sorties by way of outer
space. Understand one and we may fathom the rest.

Of course, the first step had to be a visit to Abney Hall, and
it had to be in the evening to reproduce the original circumstances.

We arrived on a cool night in late October 1988. As we turned
off the main road beside a famous private hospital we entered
a long winding driveway that took us into the interior of the Hall
grounds.

Security was non-existent. We parked beside the main building, with just the occasional light burning in its numerous
rooms and a sign that indicated it was occupied by a social
services department of Cheadle Council. Then, as the clock
struck the ominous hour of 8 p.m., we set off to circumnavigate
the building, feeling only mildly less nervous than a Renais-
sance mariner about to sail around an uncharted world.

As we skirted the forecourt to the front of Abney Hall we
found the immaculate lawn and what appeared the quintess-
ence of an English country manor house. I was more interested
in the fact that this place existed so close to my home, yet
shielded from prying eyes by the barricade of trees. I did feel
an eerie sort of atmosphere, not unlike an electrical tingling that
tickled inside. But given the story that had brought us here this
was hardly surprising.

We edged our way across the lawn towards the area where the
pond and waterfall were located. There was very little to see.
Neither Roy nor myself wished to venture further into the
undergrowth. Not because we were scared of monsters, of
course, but because it was dark and we were unsure of our
footing. At least that remains our explanation!

At the far side of the building a huge site construction was
underway, evidently creating some totally anachronistic office
block. The diggers and tractors stood in silent respect to the
night, but the arc beams and searchlights speckled through the

spook on video camera and audio tape.

However, most students of the supernatural would accept the story as it stands and treat it as a good yarn not to be spoilt by overindulgence in the sin of rational enquiry.

What position did I take? In fact neither. I knew that the circumstances were such that there was little prospect of gaining permission for any seance (however superficially technological it might appear). In any case, I have doubts that this would achieve very much, if anything at all.

Nevertheless, I did feel that the case was full of speculative insights and tiny little clues. Of course, one could never be certain that it was not a hoax. Perhaps the whole affair was a hoax, or semi-hoax born of unintended confabulation. Assuming it was honourably reported, what really mattered in my opinion was the interrelationship between the people and the area.

We know something about the people involved in the sightings, but what about Abney Hall itself? This was where my investigation focused, in an effort to learn more about the place.

It turns out that it is not a particularly ancient building. Just 180 years old, it had spent most of its life in the hands of the Watts family, wealthy cotton barons from Manchester who built it as their country retreat by the river, in the days when villages remained isolated and had not run into one another like watercolour paints on a rainy day.

The Watts were closely related by marriage to the famous mystery writer Agatha Christie, who is known to have stayed there on several occasions between the First and Second World Wars. Indeed, there is even local speculation that during the novelist's infamous and unexplained period of sudden disappearance (she eventually turned up in Harrogate without offering an acceptable reason) Ms Christie may have been at Abney Hall.

One of the Watts family is said to haunt the building, again according to local tradition. There even seems to be a rumour (largely speculation I suspect) that the female spectre in white reported by a caretaker some years ago was Agatha herself.

Certainly this unexpected connection with the queen of mystery does little to make the story easier to comprehend. I was unable to find anybody who admitted to first-hand experience of ghostly goings-on around the buildings; although I heard several tales of lights turning on and off of their own accord and guard dogs whose coats stood inexplicably on end.

After 1945 Abney Hall went out of private ownership and was used extensively as council offices for quite some time until it fell into disuse and disrepair.

Knowing that the social services department was now using the building, this became my first port of call. In fact they merely lease a small section of the building and had only done so since the previous winter.

A sympathetic official put me in touch with one of the typists who had been there since the days when it was more extensively used by Cheadle Council. However, the moment I sheepishly introduced the topic of strange goings-on, this woman, whilst denying any personal knowledge of such matters, became deeply upset. 'I don't want to know about that sort of thing,' she practically yelled at me and slammed down the 'phone.

I called straight back to speak to my more helpful contact and asked her to convey apologies for evidently terrifying her colleague. I received sympathy and understanding for my quest. Whilst this woman knew about the Agatha Christie connection and the legend of the ghost, she added very rapidly: 'But we are lucky. None of us has ever seen it. Nor do we want to.'

Following advice I moved on to the design company now occupying most of the land. I obtained many sighs of fascination but no new leads, except the mildly cynical remark that 'in a place like this you would expect that sort of story to come about'.

This company pointed out that they did not own the land and directed me to the landlords, but first I was interested in talking to those involved in the building of the new structure. The building had gone on right in the heart of the 'haunted woods' and at the time of the alleged sightings of the Ninja dwarfs. Had anything been reported by the workmen?

The contractors were alternatively amused and amazed by my revelations, although as usual I offered no details until I had milked what I could from my current contact. It appeared that almost no work was done at night or weekends and nothing strange had been observed during daylight.

1.

Myth Monsters

'I think that we are haunted,' he had said, 'by all the fantasies, all the make-believe, all the ogres that we have ever dreamed . . .'

Clifford Simak, science-fiction writer

There is nothing new about monsters. Whilst the Ninja dwarfs of Cheadle might in themselves be rather unusual, humanity has always shared the biosphere of earth with some pretty odd creatures.

Of course, questions still remain about entities as diverse as goblins, dragons, yeti, Loch Ness 'beasties' and alien humanoids. Not least we may ask whether their reality is on a concrete or psychological level.

Most of us would assume that there can be nothing more than imagination behind these myths and legends. But it is hardly that simple. Monsters have a grip on our spirit. Whilst they terrify and freeze the senses they also endure. We would each feel a strange kind of sadness if rational science could prove beyond a shadow of a doubt that none of these things had material substance. Yet who would wish to challenge them on a dark, winter's night?

That curious dichotomy, as shown by the group who were confronting the Ninja dwarfs, is typical and instructive. It suggests that we somehow *need* our monsters. That they appear to keep us sane. Indeed, I very much suspect that a clue is lurking in that sentence somewhere, but we shall return to the subject rather later. First we have some exploring to do.

ing up what he thinks to be a story out of his head at the same time as a highly imaginative person (gifted/hallucinating — choose your own word, and it will probably be wrong) is experiencing the plotline within what he calls 'reality'. Again, I am quite sure this is an important clue.

The Yorkshire pterodactyl seen briefly soaring over the glorious hills of the Pennines was innocently reported to him by some friends in a sort of 'club' of strange observers. Paul Bennet had just created a magazine entitled *Earth* to bring his new-found philosophy to a wider readership.[3] He argues that there is a kind of bond between all living, breathing consciousness on this planet and many of our mysterious phenomena emerge from that matrix.

It is the same concept coined (yet again simultaneously — in a book published in 1979) by a scientist who has written several excellent popular studies of what he came to call the 'Lifetide'.[4] This he perceives as a sea of planetary consciousness into which all souls contribute, rather like drips from a tap filling up the bathtub. It ought not to surprise us that, by another of those 'coincidences', this scientist's name is Dr Lyall *Watson*.

So, in this case we seem to have a flying dinosaur living on, not so much because it has cheated evolution, but because a science-fiction writer thought it should come to life in Yorkshire and a scientist believed it was possible. So, at the same time, a youngster collecting monsters like others might collect stamps, decides that it is *literally* possible to experience it. A curious *mental* symbiosis between all these people has occurred.

But this was not the first time that pterodactyls have stalked the skies since the last one supposedly fell to earth lifeless. Not by any means. New Jersey, USA, more than eighty years ago was the home of some frightening visitations by a flying creature which had all the hallmarks of a winged dinosaur.

The reports focused on January 1909 and involved a number of sightings of what became known as the 'Jersey Devil' — a monstrous bird with the head of a dog and face of a horse atop a long neck. Others spoke of a similarity with a kangaroo, heightened by claims that it 'hopped' leaving hoof-like prints about two and a half inches wide. But it was also seen soaring into the air on at least one occasion. This was in Bristol, Pennsylvania, and a local policeman had just tried unsuccessfully to shoot it down.

Sketches and descriptions of the bat-like wings enhance the similarity with a pterodactyl, but we may never know the truth because the intense flap of observations lasted only a week or so. During this spell, law enforcers at Riverside, New Jersey, were able to take plaster casts of the prints and there was an aborted attempt to pen it into a barn in Morrisville, Pennsylvania. Unfortunately, when the barn doors were open the 'Jersey Devil' had vanished, never to return again. [5]

Clearly something was at the heart of these reports. But it is interesting to note the way in which the small farming communities quickly became aflame with rumours about the monster. Does this suggest that a contagion effect was in operation, possibly turning some normal lifeform into a monster by a process of hysteria? Or was there an initial sighting of something very odd which lead to all the rest by a combination of misperception and suggestibility?

In the mid-sixties another part of the USA was invaded by a monstrous bird. This was around seven feet tall when erect and with its wings folded back behind it (rather like the bone structure of a pterodactyl).

Typical of the many apparitions of what became known as a 'mothman' was the encounter of the Scarberrys and the Mallettes, two couples driving near Point Pleasant, West Virginia, on 15 November 1966. They claimed that the 'thing' followed their car, despite rattling off down the highway at a frightening 100 m.p.h. Mrs Linda Scarberry commented that the most terrifying aspect of the flying entity was its eyes — red, glowing and staring right at them. (Bear this statement in mind as we will hear it again more than once in future chapters.)

Journalist and UFO sleuth John Keel became heavily involved in the case, visiting the Point Pleasant area several times during 1967. He was interested because on several occasions the 'bird' seemed to materialize out of what were originally just lights seen in the skies. These, of course, were reported as UFOs; although others suggested they were the familiar red eyes that were frequently attributed to the 'mothman'.

Keel wrote a series of progress reports for the UFO journal, *Flying Saucer Review*, and later a readable book. [6] He became fascinated with coincidences that began to link in between the

But, if you have followed my argument you should now be anxious to tell me that this is impossible. Did I not say that dinosaurs all died out long before man came to fruition?

Yes, indeed, but through our understanding of evolution we know that humans developed out of other forms of life. We owe some of our genetic make-up to mammalian creatures that *were* around when the dinosaurs roamed as the buffalo do. Indeed they were prey to the carnivorous versions of these monsters and must have had some inherent defence mechanisms and brain patterns that equated dinosaurs with danger. Possibly some of that still survives in the deeper levels of ourselves and, because all human life stems from the same source, it would be truly universal to us all and completely independent of modern nations or culture.

In a fascinating book, philosopher Arthur Koestler discussed the relationship between our brain and social behaviour.[10] Each of us has a series of brains that are built on top of one another: the reptilian brain lies beneath the mammalian brain and the human grey matter has grown around that.

Of course, most of the time we rely on the vastly superior rationalizing ability and intelligence of our human brain. But the survival instincts of the more primitive mammalian brain are still there — perhaps, I suggest, with vestiges of material about what were once vicious predators. Koestler also says that the reptilian brain is heavily emotional and is responsible for our myths and superstitions.

His highly contentious but interesting speculation is that wars, murder and sex crimes are occurring in increasing numbers because our rational human mind has developed too rapidly and is virtually out of control, like a tumour. The messages of myth, superstition and survival are still coming through from the lower level brains and these clash alarmingly with our newer organ. The schizophrenia that results produces a species insanity that is reaching the point of self-destruction.

Whether he has come up with a terrible truth or a rampant fantasy we do not yet know. However, there is something vaguely plausible about seeing those phobias and fears seep out of the primitive parts of our brain under certain circumstances to be translated by the rational, intelligent human side as an invasion by pterodactyls.

We have some evidence in support of this idea by looking at cave paintings, our best guide to how man thought tens of thousands of years ago in an age before writing was invented.

In these paintings we see many monsters, some of which could be dinosaurs. We also see apparently ordinary animals severely distorted.[11] But why is this? It is interesting to realize that our brain was then much less developed and the more primitive mammalian and reptilian sections would be in far closer contact. No higher functions were in operation to control learning, science, language etc. It is perfectly possible that material from the basement level common to us all would pour through regularly, effectively making monsters *real* to these ancient ancestors.

Even thousands of years later, when civilization was just beginning, the effect of these more primitive brain structures would probably have been considerable. This is the time when myths and legends about fabulous beasts abound, from Greek mythology to fairy tales about wild men in the woods. It could well be that perception of the world was utterly different for these people. To them such beasts had a reality status, *because* the mind was generating images of them and these were being perceived.

Are we today different only in that these images have further to go to reach the outer surface of perception or reality? And because they happen less often, and to only some of us, are we making the mistake of denying our monsters altogether?

Of course, it would be wrong to lose sight of the fact that as we have explored the world more completely we *have* found actual living monsters. It is clearly possible that more could still be awaiting discovery.

When I say that we have 'found' monsters, I mean that literally.

A hundred years ago zoologists had catalogued only a couple of thousand species of mammal. As we head towards the twenty-first century that total has expanded many fold and is now well into five figures.

Of course, most of the creatures discovered are just new varieties of those known already, with but minor differences. The discovering of a brand new species is a very rare occurrence. But it does still happen.

ness and experience a timeless, ecstatic sensation. He found it in various types of episode, including religious visions and when creativity or love is being expressed.[12]

This might seem a surreal piece of information of little relevance, but it is another of those facts to store away for later consideration when it will be seen to be important.

This sense of being 'at one with the universe' is especially prevalent in young children, where time has a different meaning anyway. A week lasts an eternity and next year is an unthinkable distance away. Summers drift on endlessly and winter nights are dark, cold and frightening.

This cannot be mere idle philosophy. In some real sense it is a truth. Our perception of time *does* alter in a very real manner as we grow older.

So the magical state of consciousness of a child is quite specific. It is a time we can all remember, because we have all lived through it. We know the difference between our last Christmas as a child and our first as an adult. Only twelve months spanned the gulf, but we might as well have been two different people living in opposing universes. The loss of the sparkle, excitement, belief in fairy tales and our wondrous innocence hits us terribly hard. Of course, there are compensations which come from growing older and seeing the world 'as it really is' (or rather as others *teach* us it really is). But who amongst us would not trade back for those days when we were six or seven years old?

In that first 10 per cent of our lifetime we have no concept of responsibilities, of paying bills, needing to be somewhere by the clock and most of the rest of what comes to dominate the remainder of our days. Instead, we gladly submit to a reality which sees the universe as a miracle, which accepts that forces outside of us can weave spells and where monsters of all kinds are ready to pounce if we misbehave.

Seen from our unsteady perch on the ragged rocks of rationality these days will probably appear naive and embarrassing to most of us. We even use the term 'childish' in a derogatory fashion. However, all that has taken place is the learning of a new set of ground rules — not necessarily a better set or a more correct appreciation of the world, just a different one.

In pre-school and early post-school days we had an utterly unique way of thinking and believing. It conditioned our reality.

It *was* our reality. It was no less true for us then than the world we believe in now is true — true, because our textbooks *tell* us we should believe in it.

One thing that strikes me about children is the way they accept the paranormal. A very large number of young people undergo strange experiences, be they 'out of the body' sensations, or dreams about the future, or seeing strange things in the sky. As we become adult we learn that such things do not happen. Science says they are impossible. So we shift them into a cellar of our mind, where they grow cobwebs and are forgotten. Or we run away from our memories and abilities for fear that we transgress some terrible law of nature by having these experiences.

It is perfectly possible that children have more paranormal experiences, not because they are gullible and have yet to learn what they should properly believe, but rather because they are open-minded and perceptive and have yet to be taught what they must *disbelieve*.

At Stanford University in the USA, psychologist Ernest Hilgard was especially interested in the 'imaginary companions' claimed by children, particularly before the age of six. He found that a very surprising number (between 15 and 20 per cent of all youngsters) did have regular communication with people who were very real to them, but whom nobody else saw. However, if questioned later in life, most of these children forgot about such things because it was part of what our new-found adult status insists we must regard as imaginative nonsense.

Another American psychologist, Dr Thomas Armstrong, has studied the various stages through which young children pass *without* making these sweeping assumptions, i.e. that experiences of the imagination have no reality.[13]

A combination of Armstrong's work and Hilgard's research into imaginary playmates illustrates an interesting pattern.

In the earliest (youngest) phase, called the *prepersonal*, children usually imagine monsters of the devouring kind. Speculation is that this reflects the bond with the mother and the child's origin in the womb.

Next comes the *subpersonal* stage, where the common motif amongst imagined companions is of 'little people' or invisible spirits and forces. The theory here is that this compares with the child seeing himself as a tiny being lost in a vast universe with unimaginable forces in control. This is typical just as he is about to start school.

The child then enters what is called the *personal* level, where the playmates are 'real' people who simply do not exist in the strict sense of the word and have been 'created' in order to help him or her understand the world of social interactions (as children must do in a school environment).

Finally, there is the *suprapersonal* experience where the predominant type of imagined companion is the spiritual master, usually with flowing robes and wise messages. Today we recognize these easily as the alien mentors in close encounter cases. This is typical around the age of six.

We can examine many classic stories of 'imaginary' contact and place them within one or other of these frameworks. The Brontë sisters, for example, created an entire world of people which later became the characters in their stories. Enid Blyton, on the other hand, based most of her children's stories about strange beings on dramas that acted themselves out in front of her eyes; whereas the children at the centre of the Lourdes or Fatima religious 'miracles' had visits from glowing spiritual figures that nobody else was able to see.

We can find similar examples where fairies, little people or aliens have been seen and are still being seen by young children. Clearly the phases of development which these psychologists propose *are* valid.

But what if we extend this concept to humanity as a whole? Have we gone through similar stages as a species down through the millenia and as our brain power has become ever more sophisticated? There is good reason to see a very evident analogy and it must be more than coincidence. After all, humanity is made up of human beings, and if individual humans show this pattern of development in their lives, then surely our species should follow the trend also.

Let us think through how this might manifest itself.

The first phase would involve beasts and monsters and devouring images — the sort of stuff that peppers the walls of cave artists and mythology, suggesting that these merely reflect the *prepersonal* stage of human development, the one that accompanied the 'dawn' of man.

If we look at what should come next, then we find that in the *subpersonal* there is a concentration on little people and outside forces, which seems to fit in perfectly with most of our history as a species right through towards the late Middle Ages when science began to take command.

We should now be able to predict the next stage, the *personal*, where real but imagined people are at the core. Does that not equate neatly with the development of spiritualism in the last century, when mediums began to make contact with real people in supposed other dimensions of existence?

Had we looked at this half a century ago we might have noted the way in which the stages were becoming of shorter duration as our species seemed to progress at a frightening and escalating pace. We could then have predicted the consequences of the *suprapersonal* phase, with its theme of wise beings with spiritual powers way beyond our own. It is fascinating to see that this is precisely what has transpired in human society, with the recent growth in alien contacts of just this sort.

If we take these stages as symptomatic of our growth as a human spirit, then it is immediately apparent that we are at a crucial point. For after the *suprapersonal* stage the child 'grows up' and denies all that made him young in a new rush of objectivity.

Is that where mankind is headed next? Are we about to enter our teenage years as a civilization, adopting whole new responsibilities and going through the powerful process we know as puberty?

In a young person, the change towards adult status via puberty is always a painful one, with dramatic physical and psychological upheavals. If our species really is about to go through its own cultural puberty then that time must be very near and surely cannot occur without dramatic consequences.

Whatever else may be won or lost, the individual is forever altered by this period of transition. I wonder if the same will be true for humanity and just how different our society may be a century from now.

Another indicator of our progress is literature, which develops in parallel with our species.

When writers enter a creative mode they are really tapping into the deep subconscious mind and dredging out material which may reflect universal beliefs. This is well illustrated by studying the Gothic novels of the last century.[14]

From Mary Shelley's *Frankenstein* we see the idea that if science tries to reduce life to nothing but material experimentation, it may unleash the monster inside us all. That sets into fictional context the debate that was about to erupt over Darwinian theories of evolution. Were we more than mere animals? Could our soul survive intact through the triumph of science?

Then came Robert Louis Stevenson and *Dr Jekyll and Mr Hyde*, which was even more explicit in its insight into our 'dual' brain which may allow animal impulses to surge forth. Indeed, when it was being presented as a play in London during 1888, the infamous 'Jack the Ripper' killings typified the same theme of a crazed killer who was undetectable because most of the time he was just an ordinary man. Indeed, so similar was the cruel reality to the dramatic fiction that the leading actor became a suspect and the play was eventually taken off. It was too horribly accurate.

A few years later there was a spate of vampire and dracula novels which now sought to personify the monster side of us as a being which is almost human but sufficiently removed from humanity to be easier to handle. During the late 1890s and early 1900s, as this theme became common, London was hit by apparitions of what was called 'Spring Heeled Jack' — a vampire-like man in a cloak whose main trademark was to leap about and practically 'fly' through the air. People 'really' *were* seeing these things.

The being was said to be tall, wore a helmet and had clawed animal-like hands that scythed at his victims' faces. As late as September 1904 there were sightings of 'Jack' in the Everton district of Liverpool, where he was reported to be leaping from rooftop to rooftop. Even in 1975 researcher Andy Collins followed up a case in the East End of London where a youngster reported seeing a figure that glowed red and could spring from one pavement to another right across the end of a terraced street. The legend of Jack persists even today.

What we see here are examples of how literature and the real world simultaneously conjure up the same motif that seems to be spelling something out — just as we found with the pterodactyl encounters in 1978.

More clues emerge when we learn that Mary Shelley's *Frankenstein* in 1818 was based on a dream; so too was *Dr Jekyll and Mr Hyde*. These further demonstrate the subconscious store from whence the writers' images emerged.

All early forms of science fiction used the monster theme before becoming more sophisticated and using beings from other worlds. At first, even these were always monsters (as evidenced by most of the famous sci-fi movies of the fifties). It is a recent trend that has seen the move towards wise beings of advanced spiritual awareness that we find in movies such as *Close Encounters of the Third Kind*.[15]

We can also find a number of small aspects of these 'invented' stories which frequently crop up in real monster cases, such as glowing eyes, a sulphurous smell and time suspension during the encounter. Others will occur to us as we look at some of the case histories in this book.

This all should warn that the relationship between fact and fiction is not so much a sharp dividing line as a curious blend of mutual interaction.

In order to summarize some of the points made in this chapter it would be opportune to give a few examples of actual sightings.

A typical case from just before the pre-modern era was investigated by Dr Michele Clare and occurred in Rotherham, South Yorkshire, during the winter of 1937.

The witness, Robert, was walking his dog along a dark lane near one of the coal pits that dot the area when he observed a strange figure running down a steep slope. It was evening, and dark, but the behaviour of the figure was recognizable as most unusual because it ran straight at a fence and went *through* it as if nothing were there.

This might at first sound like some sort of ghost story, except that the being passed within inches of Robert and was plainly not human (dead or alive). It was only just over five feet tall, covered in hair and had claw-like hands and feet. The head also appeared to be pointed. The figure continued its mad dash straight towards the railway line heading into Sheffield, and Robert's dog decided it had had enough and bolted home.

The description of the entity was rather like that of a popularized visitor from Hades: 'You look as if you've seen the devil!'

his mother exclaimed when she first saw Robert's ashen face.
'I have,' was all Robert need reply.

This simple story illustrates the common theme of animal
reaction (as if animals 'sense' things we do not) and also shows
one of the problems of interpretation in such cases. Robert had
his own views on who or what the figure was. Others would
have formed the conclusion it was a spectre, whilst a couple of
decades later the press would have been looking for the spaceship out of which the 'alien' had emerged.[16]

We can update this story to the space age very easily by
looking at the case of Gary, now an engineer at Chicago's O'Hare
Airport, one of the busiest terminals in the world. He wrote to
tell me of his experiences when in his late teens.

It was in the winter of 1978. Gary was living in Illinois and
standing by the bathroom window when 'suddenly a light in
the corner caused me to stare at it. A white, round, completely
unbelievable form slowly emerged through the no-see-through
glass. It came just inside the inner pane and said "Boo" — then
slowly retreated back out and was gone.'

One is tempted to smile at such a story, especially when we
examine Gary's sketch of the vapourish face, round eyes that
glowed red and the peculiar mouth. However, this was only one
experience amidst many others. Gary has gone through a lifetime of seeing strange things in the skies around Chicago and
inside his bedroom, including some quite frightening monster
apparitions. His evaluation of these encounters is, almost inevitably, that he has been abducted by space aliens. In 1987, when
he first wrote to me, that was the 'in vogue' solution in the USA.
But is that true in any *real* sense, or just the contemporary
evaluation of a much longer standing problem?

To him these things are real, and that is what counts. But note
here the interesting idea that the monstrous form materialized
out of a patch of misty light. It emerged from nothing by way
of an amorphous blob.

Much more traditional monsters were seen by a woman who
wrote to me about her many and varied adventures. By profession she is an astrologer and her experiences include everything
from 'standing up and feeling that there were two of me, and not
being sure which was the real me' (probably a relevant observation) to a meeting in Swiss Cottage, London that Robert from

Rotherham would have found familiar. Here she met 'a man in a red track suit, tall and dark and looking rather like the old pictures of the devil'.

However, amidst these many visions of unusual forms the most interesting reported by our astrologer took place in May 1972 when she was on a coach tour of Eastern Europe.

It was in the middle of the night and she was somewhere near Posen in Poland. Ahead of her a sister coach was travelling the same homebound route. All occupants of both vehicles were asleep. Suddenly: 'I saw a group of "Gremlins" on the roof of the bus. They were the size of a child aged seven or eight, but very human in appearance, yet obviously not human.'

She describes these fugitives from a Steven Spielberg movie as 'not quite solid, yet not transparent' and gleefully playing about on the roof, aware that the humans right below them had no understanding they were there. Whilst she tried to persuade herself that she was 'hallucinating' she continued to see them for many minutes. The driver of her coach, who was (presumably!) awake, apparently saw nothing and she never mentioned the figures to him. Her view is that she was specially attuned to being able to observe these monsters, whereas others were not.[17]

We might speculate endlessly about some sort of experience on the edge between wakefulness and sleep (where vivid hallucinations are not uncommon). Also I think we gain interesting insights into her perception of reality when we learn that earlier the same night (on the road between Smolensk and Moscow) she says the bus was followed by a UFO. Yet, from what we can gather about the date and the time, and her description of this object evaluated as a 'spaceship', it might well have been the moon, which was full on the 28 May 1972, low on the horizon and in the right position.

But how does somebody fail to recognize an object as familiar as the moon? The answer to that question is yet another that is probably important.

Sometimes the object that is involved in the encounter is very ambiguous and interpretation of what it may be is imposed from outside. This is much more likely to happen in this day and age of media hysteria where in order to sell a story we have to pin a label on it first.

Two cases in 1988 demonstrate this well.

Just before 5 a.m. on the summer's morning of 20 January 1988 the Knowles family were driving their 1984 Ford along the Eyre Highway between Perth and Adelaide in southern Australia. According to the testimony of Mrs Faye Knowles and her three sons, including Sean (the driver), a white glow first appeared in the east. Then, before they knew what was happening, the egg-like mass was directly above them and Sean was struggling to retain control. Mrs Knowles put her hand through the open window and felt a spongey texture to the blob floating invisibly above their heads. Sean, now speeding to get away, burst a tyre and the Ford screeched to a halt.

Leaping from the car they fled to a bush beside the road, with the invisible 'thing' still nearby and humming. A foul stench had invaded the car with a black mist, which they assumed came from the thing that followed them, and it was some minutes before they had the composure to come out of hiding, see that the mass had gone, change tyres and drive on to the police station at Ceduna.

Excellent and rapid investigation was carried out by Ray Brooke and others of a local investigation team (UFORA). Whilst the sincerity of the family was obvious and something clearly had distressed them, analysis of the physical evidence (e.g. the black ash left in the car) proved inconclusive, as this turned out to be quite like worn brake-lining.

Of much more concern was the response of the media. One TV company intercepted the car on the family's way home from the police, signed them up with lucrative offers and soon the case became a major international story. The car was taken over for a 'tour' by an entrepeneur. Signposts warning motorists of low flying UFOs appeared and front page reports on the case were in papers all over the world within 24 hours. The Knowles family were not really to blame. It is the way of the supernatural world.

The dark mass was now clearly identified as a 'UFO', the car had been 'attacked' and 'driven off the road' and the whole story began to lose itself amidst its own exaggerations. Over in Britain, the tabloids wrote it up in graphic detail, e.g. the *Daily Star*'s 'UFO hijack terror' and the even more specific *Daily Mirror* headline 'The pong from outer space'.

There was absolutely no justification for spaceship or even UFO interpretations, but they sell newspapers and today that is often all that matters. The truth about the case became virtually impossible to disentangle from the media hype that surrounded it. Yet all the Knowles family saw was a big blob that in other circumstances and other eras might have been regarded as a gremlin, demon or even a pterodactyl![18]

Just six weeks later a similar thing took place in rural Cambridgeshire. It was just after teatime on 2 March 1988 and a 14-year-old girl named Pauline had been in the garden of her Godmanchester home, mucking out her pets and listening to the radio. Suddenly a faint roar began, grew to a loud vibrating noise and a terrible odour, described as akin to rotten eggs (hydrogen sulphide) struck her nostrils from out of the blue. A small black mass was floating by and Pauline — wisely — fled inside.

Once again the story became exaggerated as it was written up. Without realizing how these facts would be popularized, Pauline and her family spoke honestly about what had transpired, leading to stories such as 'Tea bag UFO zaps Pauline' (*The Sun*).

The most disturbing effect of all this was that Pauline spent weeks off school, terrified of the reaction of her school chums. Not surprisingly many regarded the story as most things, but rarely as the literal truth. Indeed I was ultimately contacted by Pauline's educational welfare officer who wanted my advice on how to try to resolve this situation and find a way to get Pauline back into a normal life.[19]

Again, through no fault of the witness, but because of our lust for exciting monster yarns and the manner in which the story was sensationalized, potentially long-term damage was done to a young girl's life.

I cannot see any excuse for such behaviour. But it happens, and will continue to happen, because we regard such encounters as fair game for frivolity. Instead of recognizing that people are having genuine experiences for which we have no simple solution, and treating them to assessment and analysis in an effort to find such a solution, we impugn the credibility of those involved. Then, instead of seeking answers through reasonable and responsible debate, we discuss the matter alongside trivia and titillation only in the sort of medium that regards the supernatural as a sales-marketing ploy.

Monsters are real, even in this day and age. But they are far more dangerous to our minds and our society irrespective of what *kind* of reality they possess. They are dangerous because we cannot take them seriously.

2.

Water Monsters

Absence of evidence is not evidence of absence.

Dr Martin Rees, sceptical scientist

An alien visitor viewing our solar system from outer space would find it most peculiar that we have chosen to call our planet 'earth'. They would see it is not made up of rock and soil, but dominated by the rich, enticing blue of the oceans. These swamp our world. Indeed, all life (including our own) would not last more than a few days but for this overwhelming ratio in favour of water. Surely any intelligent race discovering our tiny abode would come up with a name more befitting than the one we have invented?

Of course, we use the term because we are land dwellers. In doing so we forget that we owe our origins to the seas and that far more forms of life exist within those depths than we ever witness in our lifetimes.

In short, water holds many mysteries, including several species with an intelligence that may be equal to our own (whales and dolphins). We are remarkably ignorant and dismissive of such facts.

But it was not always this way. Since ancient times the miraculous power of water has been well understood. Every body of any substantial size was afforded the protection of an invisible guardian spirit (or sprite). It is possible that this owes something to the reality of water's invigorating effect. The generation of ozone creates ionization and in earlier days we may have been more aware of the tickling sensations ionization produces, and we may have sought to dramatize them as secret powers.

From this background comes many legends of monsters. In the days when the only means of travelling any distance, especially from island civilizations, was by the dangerous route of an ocean crossing, stories of powerful beasts inhabiting the depths grew freely.

Sometimes these tales were used to ward off potential invaders. On other occasions they were mere fables, playing on our desire to be tantalized and frightened. Occasionally they were real reports of creatures that lived so far out of sight below the waves that we rarely caught a glimpse of them and never twice in any lifetime. Without cameras to offer proof only storytelling could preserve these creatures for future generations.

However, not all strange water-creatures belong to the days when ancient explorers were daring to cross treacherous seas in search of new lands and treasure trove. Some come from our own microwave and TV society.

The Isle of Man, midway between the English and Irish coasts, is a wonderful place to visit. Rich in Norse history and fairy glades it also has long traditions of association with the sea. Surrounded as it is (indeed from its peaks you can see every country in the United Kingdom on a clear day) this is inevitable.

But in March 1961 nobody could have anticipated that a mermaid would be seen off its rocky coast; and seen not by some drunken sailor, but no less a personage than the lady mayoress of the town of Peel.[20]

Of course, we assume that she must have been mistaken. The usual explanation offered by science is that the 'mermaid' was a seal grazing on the shoreline. Yet seals are commonplace around the island. How could a native make such an error? The figure was reputedly that of a humanoid on top and a fish below waist level. We can speculate about misty conditions and distance, but we still ponder.

Although most mermaids throughout the centuries have probably been manatees — seal-like creatures with whiskers, breasts and surprisingly human skin and fingers — this cannot be true of the sighting off Peel. Nor can it be true of any of the other reports from around the shores of Britain, as the manatee lives only in tropical waters.

Back in the Isle of Man, and true to form, the tourist board recognized the publicity value of the report and offered a reward should their mermaid be captured alive. So far as I know it never was, but this has hardly stopped mermaids (and mermen) still being seen all over the world, for they are one of the most consistent and widespread of monster apparitions. Whilst they may not sound particularly terrifying, they were often blamed for luring sailors to their doom on the rocks.

In June 1987 I took a bus across America from Washington DC, bound for Chicago. Americans are a talkative folk and I had the charming company of a professional musician. He was making an expedition to Lake Tahoe, on the Nevada/California border. Here he would entertain the customers during the long, hot summer in this popular resort.

Lake Tahoe, it transpired (and much to my surprise) has its own water monster, something I had to check up on in order to satisfy myself that I was not being told a modern traveller's tale to while away the roadbound hours.

This lake is deep (more than a quarter of a mile). On 19 June 1984 two young hikers (who turned out to be Patsy McKay and Diane Stavarkis from the nearby town of Tahoe City) observed what they first took to be a sinking boat on the surface of the waters. However, it turned out to be a 'hump' (almost 20 feet long) that was moving around in a circle, going beneath the surface and then coming up again. This created the sort of impression that a whale might when much of its body is masked underwater. (Needless to say a whale was not the cause of this report in a freshwater lake many miles inland from the Pacific Ocean.)

The UPI press agency reported this case and other subsequent claims of similar objects seen, including witnesses who were actually on the lake at the time of their encounter.

According to *Fortean Times*, who collect strange press items from all over the world in the spirit of their mentor Charles Fort, the sightings were preceded by local rumours about an aquatic monster in the area. Certainly, once the media got hold of the account it grew precisely like the proverbial fisherman's tale.

The *US Sun*, a fun-loving tabloid, was soon discussing the

monster that was said to be 100 feet long with huge jaws and which left webbed footprints on the sandy shore. It even quoted a newly married couple staying locally as having seen a creature 'black in color' with 'scales like a snake' which was, in their words (or rather the words the newspaper say they used) 'as tall as a ten-storey building'.[21]

Having seen examples of how the media engage in myth making during the last chapter, we should recognize some of the symptoms. All the Lake Tahoe beast needs now is a pleasant sounding name with vaguely un-nerving associations and a great new legend can develop. How about the 'Tahoe Terror'?

Nessie, the Scottish beastie from Loch Ness, is familiar all over the world. It is a classic illustration of how a tourist boom industry has grown up around a possibly non-existent myth. But it by no means stands alone. Virtually every lake of any size in a line through this part of the northern hemisphere has its own undiscovered inhabitant. They just have not been used quite as effectively as their Scottish counterpart.

Janet and Colin Bord compiled a list of lakes in Wales and Ireland with such a legend and it reads like a tourist brochure of some of the more popular spots (e.g. Lough Derg in County Donegal, plus the largest inland lake in Britain, Lough Neagh, and Llyn Cynwch in Gwynedd).

Morag, the creature said to inhabit Loch Morar, is almost as famous in Scotland as its nearby cousin. Described as dirty brown in colour, with three humps, between 20 and 30 feet long, rough skin and a serpentine head, it is very similar to Nessie and even sports a fairly unexciting photograph, taken on 31 January 1977 by a young woman who saw a small rock-like protrusion break the surface.[22]

North American lakes have plenty of monster associations. Champ is the delightful name given to the typical humped creature in Lake Champlaine and Ogopogo and Chessie are other favourites from northerly latitudes. A few distant photographic images have been captured of some of these creatures, all of which bear considerable likeness to one another.

Rodney Davis carried out a fascinating study of the creature said to inhabit Lake Pohenegamook, which straddles the border between Maine in the USA and Quebec in Canada.[23]

It seems that Ponik is the name given to this particular mon-

Alleged lake monster, approximately a dozen feet in length, filmed by two fishermen, Richard Vincent and John Konefell. They were on Lake Manitoba in Canada on 12 August 1962 and the snake-like creature reportedly outswam their motorized boat with a 'rippling' motion (*Fortean Picture Library*).

ster which, according to figures worked out by Davis, has been seen fifty times since the last century.

Typical of his reports is the sighting by Leo Quellette in May 1961, who was on the lake in his canoe when he saw the thing as a dark mass with two humps breaking the surface.

Not everyone has been convinced that Ponik exists, although descriptions are very consistent at around 25 feet long, black or dark brown coloration and a 'saw-tooth fin' along its back. However, Dr Vadim Vladikov, a biologist from Ottawa University, angered the locals by studying the stories and coming away convinced it was a giant sturgeon that had accidentally been released into the pool.

How this fairly mundane fish had survived out of the sea and for a century or more was not explained. But other solutions included seals swimming in formation and gas bubbles floating to the surface from vegetation at the base of the lake. Of course, nothing would kill off the belief in the monster now it was a part of local heritage.

Dr Vladikov's strange idea may not be as far fetched as it seems. There were many similar stories about a monster at Stafford Lake, near Novato, California. In this case the stories do not seem to have referred to a monster as large as 25 feet, or one with several humps. But rumours always lead to exaggerations and the sightings inevitably became more fascinating.

In August 1984 it finally proved possible to resolve this mystery in a unique way. Because of necessary repairs to a dam, the entire lake was temporarily drained. And, lo, there really *was* a monster at the bottom. Indeed, it was captured alive and transported to a marine aquarium in nearby San Francisco.[24]

The monster which had given rise to all these tales would have been familiar to the Ottawa biologist. It was a huge sturgeon, weighing in at 150 lb and with an impressive length of over seven feet. Its age was such that it would have been fully grown in the lake for half a century at least, so could very easily have generated the legend that it did. Perhaps Lake Pohenegamook may yet reveal a similar explanation one day.

It is quite rare for a water monster to be caught, but there are other occasions when this has happened.

Mark Chorvinsky from Rockville, Maryland, is one of the leading investigators into water-monster stories. He edits his own fine magazine, which produces up to date reports. He has also initiated the International Monster Database, an ambitious project to correlate all known sightings by way of a computer.[25]

Chorvinsky has shown a special interest in cases where dead bodies purported to be monsters have turned up. But, as he says: 'Unfortunately, most unusual carcasses turn out to have prosaic explanations.'[26]

Typical of the cases he cites is the 35 ton serpent-like creature beached at Tecoluta, Mexico, in March 1969. It had many features that made it look like a sea monster, and sported a ten-foot long tusk, as might be found on an elephant, sticking out of its head. The world media had a field day discussing prehistoric beasts and so forth. But on 20 April that year a team of scientists concluded that it was just a whale (although whales are not known to possess tusks, of course).

The badly-decomposing and foul-smelling body was ordered

for rapid burial by the scientists, but the mayor of Tecoluta decided that the number of people flocking to his humble town to see the thing ought to be rewarded and refused to commit the remains to the ground.

On 25 April 1977 the crew of a Japanese trawler, the *Zuiyo Maru*, hauled in a most unusual catch off the coast to the east of Christchurch, New Zealand — a rotting dead 'sea serpent' with a long neck and which was 33 feet in overall length. Little was visible of the original form of the beast, but the superstitious sailors needed no persuading of what now lay draped unceremoniously across their decks. There was only one place they wanted this monster to be, and that was back in the ocean.

Fortunately they took some photographs of the monstrosity first, but that did little to resolve the problem. The animal had been dead about a month, according to its state of extreme decay, and all that was left, after the effects of the ocean and predators, was a mangled white mess, barely recognizable as a once living creature.

Speculation raged. There was even a conference of scientists convened in Tokyo that autumn. But whilst sketches of what the beast *might* have looked like were generated, precise identification did not prove possible. There were suggestions it might have been a (truly) giant turtle and most seemed to favour an unknown species of shark. (When flesh strips away from sharks after death they can create a wholly misleading impression of a long, gangling neck.) But the truth is that nobody was certain and the New Zealand sea monster remains one of the few possible captures of such an alleged animal.[27]

However, by far the most important case of a deceased marine creature of unknown origin is that first reported to the May 1986 edition of the BBC *Wildlife* magazine. The claim came from Essex naturalist Owen Burnham, whose story was explored in detail by zoologist Karl Shuker, and with quite extraordinary consequences.[28]

Burnham was on holiday with his family in the Gambia, on the west coast of Africa. At approximately 8.30 a.m. on the morning of 12 June 1983 he came across two natives in the process of decapitating a dead animal. This creature was almost fully intact and was spreadeagled on the beach. Unhappily, Burnham did not have a camera to film this monster, but he took extensive notes and made excellent sketches of what he and two other family members observed.

The creature was somewhat like an elongated porpoise, about 16 feet in total length. On the top its smooth skin was brown and underneath it was white. It had two sets of flippers, although the rear ones were damaged. There were also 80 teeth, a long beak but no blowholes to indicate it was a mammal such as a new form of whale.

When Burnham asked the natives what they called the creature they said it was a dolphin, but there is no chance of this being an accurate explanation if his description and sketches are even remotely correct.

As part of his major exploration of this case, zoologist Shuker compared the creature with every possible form of living sea animal. None gave a match up ratio for major body features of much more than one in three. However, when he extended this study to *extinct* creatures the situation changed dramatically.

Easily the most significant match for the Gambian monster was found with extinct marine crocodiles of quite prodigious length known as pliosaurs, a family of short-necked plesiosaurs, for which the last known fossils are 70 million years old.

The entire type of marine dinosaur is universally considered to have been extinct since that era, although the coelacanth was in exactly the same position on the evolution record. No fossils of that five-foot long fish have been found between 70 million years and now, but it is very much alive. However, it took fifty years after that 1938 breakthrough capture mentioned previously to film a *living* colony in the Indian Ocean, producing the remarkable discovery that the coelacanth has four finny limbs and can almost be said to 'walk' on them like a dinosaur probably did![29]

These similarly 'extinct' long-necked plesiosaurs are remarkably reminiscent of most lake-monster sightings where the head and flippers are seen and the neck can bend to give the various humps. That an 89.3 per cent match-up was found in the detailed anatomical comparison between their short-necked cousins and the Gambian sea monster is to say the least incredible.

Assuming Burnham and Shuker are being honest, and their abilities as naturalists and observers are as good as they appear, there seems to be little room left to argue against the probability that a dinosaur did wash up on an African beach in 1983.

Africa and Australia are alike in some respects. Both are large landmasses with plenty of unexplored bush and jungle in the interior. Both have indigenous native populations with traditions spanning back thousands of years that are largely passed on by word of mouth. Some of this tradition relates to unknown animals.

However, where they differ most is in Australia's isolation. This isolation has always fascinated students of the earth's fauna because it virtually allowed species to develop in that continent as if it were another planet, cut off not by the ocean of space but by the natural aquatic ones.

We are all familiar with some of the more pleasing examples, such as the kangaroo, wallaby and wombat. They do not have twins anywhere else on earth, although certain Australian species do. This is partly due to what is called 'parallel evolution', where the same sort of processes in two differing locations pass through more or less the same stages to create practically identical lifeforms that are equally equipped to cope. Another factor is that during the glacial periods land bridges did exist from time to time, allowing species to migrate from and to Australia to some extent.

Rex Gilroy as curator of the Mount York Natural History Museum in New South Wales has been fascinated by aboriginal tales of giant reptiles said to still exist deep in the Australian bush. He has led expeditions inland from Queensland in an effort to verify these stories. As he reports in *Fortean Times*, he has not yet succeeded, but 'throughout the many years that I have spent researching strange animals throughout Australia and the Pacific region I have gathered a vast number of such reports.'[30]

These accounts are quite terrifying, coming as they do from swampy areas and referring to beasts said to be 30 feet long and with powerful legs and thick tails. A good view was had, for instance, by herpetologist Frank Gordon, travelling through the Wattagan Mountains in a Land Rover early in 1979. Having stopped by a swamp where he was looking for skinks he was just about to drive away when he saw a strange 'log' on the embankment next to him. The 'log' became even stranger when it rose up and scuttled into the trees.

The description of this lizard-like beast is generally of an enormous version of the monitor — greyish with stripes or bands across its body. One witness even claims he saw the thing devouring a cow.

It does seem that in the few remaining inaccessible parts of our world there are some grounds for suspecting that a few genuine monsters might be roaming.

Whilst Rex Gilroy has so far failed to find his prey and points out we shall never known for certain 'until we are able to examine either a skeleton, a fresh carcass or a living specimen', elsewhere the quest has been a little more fruitful.

Of course, by far the most hunted water monster has to be that of Loch Ness, where barely a year goes by without some new scientific expedition endeavouring to find it. Loch Ness has not only the advantage of fame, but also a reasonably small size and proximity to civilization. However, the 1,000 feet deep waters are filled with fine, suspended particles of peat and it is almost impossible to see more than a few inches under the surface. The intrepid underwater explorer Jacques Cousteau said, for instance, that he would not contemplate working in that environment.

This drawback has been the greatest stumbling block to success, even though casual thought about the question implies that if real creatures were within the Loch they would have already provided the proof we need.

But is this so? And indeed what *have* all these years of effort achieved other than dismal failure?

Dismal failure is certainly the conclusion of arch monster-debunker Steuart Campbell. A fervent Scottish nationalist he even refused to call the beast anything other than N in his research and the Loch became just L. Ness, because non-Gaelic speakers do not understand that language!

Such idiosyncrasies aside, and assuming we can overcome this introduction to his book without being tempted to dismiss him as a crank, then there is no doubt that Campbell has raised some very serious questions about the lack of hard evidence from the Loch. He demonstrates that there are many processes of mistaken identity which give rise to false monster sightings, from floating logs to solitary boat wakes that appear many minutes *after* the vessel has passed by. And he has to my mind adequately refuted some of the most impressive photographic evidence, including that widely regarded as the best which was taken by surgeon Robert Wilson near Invermoriston on 19 April 1934. There seems little doubt, after Campbell's studious analysis, that the head and neck of 'Nessie' on that print cannot have been more than a foot or two in size and that it was very likely a diving otter that accidentally appeared monster-like on the film. [31]

Many of the other famous photographs seem less impressive in the light of sober research. If we look in an entirely new way at the so-called threshing monster taken by Hugh Gray at Foyers in November 1933, I suspect we will never see it as a monster again.

Photograph taken on 12 November 1933 by Hugh Gray at Loch Ness. Said at the time to be a 'snake-like' monster around 40 feet in length it takes on a whole new dimension when you look at it according to the instructions in the text . . . Do you still see a monster?

Let us imagine that it is a dog with a stick in its mouth swimming towards the camera. Almost everyone instantly sees a very different photograph when they impose that interpretation on the image.

In fact, it does not really matter whether this photograph is genuine, a deliberate hoax or an accidental one (although if this is a dog it is difficult to imagine the cameraman did not see it approach). What is truly important is that our perception of the blur on this photograph changes when we change our expectation.

View it as a monster and we can indeed see the long, sinuous body of Nessie. Now switch to the interpretation of it as a dog holding a stick, blurred and faint because of its motion during the time exposure, and instantly the picture changes.

This flipping of 'reality' is not unlike certain optical illusions where an act of will imposes an entirely new version of what the illusion represents onto an image we have otherwise regarded quite differently. It shows how expectation, belief systems and conscious mental acts literally forge reality as we experience it.

The dog may be an entirely spurious creation of the light and shade on the picture. But once our mind accepts the photograph that way then it no longer sees the monstrous interpretation.

The Hugh Gray photograph is, in my opinion, very possibly the most signficant 'paranormal' image ever captured, because it encapsulates the human dimension of not just the Loch Ness beast, but every other monster and most anomalous phenomena too.

In other words, we *see* an ambiguous image — in this case a fuzzy blur. We are told (or know because we are witnesses at the scene) the location and context. In this case, just knowing the photograph comes from Loch Ness is enough. Instantly, just as if we were interpreting ink blots in a psychiatrist's surgery, we arrange the image according to our expectations and re-create a monster before our eyes. However, when somebody else points out a different interpretation that we have never thought of, then we swiftly alter our perception. At least we do if we are rational open-minded people *without* the need to convince ourselves that the monster truly exists.

I have seen this operate in other circumstances. Look at the UFO picture, taken in May 1975. Know only that it was taken by a responsible witness from Rochdale, Lancashire, out of his bedroom window. He said that it 'looks like a UFO'.

Indeed it does. We see a crescent or 'hang glider' shape in the sky above the houses. Now add the knowledge that the witness was a police officer. Think about his helmet with a bright badge on the front catching the sun and reflecting strongly. Now look at the 'UFO' again and I think you will start to see it as a police-man's helmet tossed into the air and frozen by the camera shutter in a slightly odd angular pose.

I do not know the truth here. Despite being challenged on this the witness never admitted it *was* a helmet, or a hoax. In fact I had the photograph several years myself before somebody pointed out this interpretation to me and ever since then my concept of the 'reality' of the Rochdale photograph has altered. I have found it hard not to 'see' it in this much more mundane way.

I suspect that this is of crucial importance in our under-standing of monsters. Very possibly an ordinary stimulus seen in a somewhat unusual or ambiguous circumstance can 'be-come' something that is strange and puzzling in a very real sense

This photograph was taken by a police officer, who wishes to remain anonymous. He alleges that he was cleaning his camera in the bedroom of his Rochdale, Lancashire, home in May 1975 when this object (shaped like a bird or hang-glider) flew over. Again, if you read the instructions (see pages 53-4) you may now interpret this photograph somewhat differently; although the witness still considers it unexplained (*MUFORA*).

of that term. If our cultural and social conditioning allows for a monster to be present in that lake, or a UFO to be flying those skies, then that is how most of us will tend to rationalize what is going on. It is just human nature.

Of course, we do not often have photographs that might ultimately decide the issue. Usually, it comes down to what eyewitnesses describe. If they go through the above process then their *memory* of their *perception* of *reality* all combine to produce a seemingly first-class observation. A monster-sighting emerges from what may not have been the same strength of perceptual data which the dramatic impact of the end-product might have suggested.

Naturally, this does not apply in all cases. It does not have a great deal of bearing on carcasses (although even here there may be a tendency to see what we expect to find in rotted remains). It has less to say about the few photographs or other 'hard' evidence we possess, which is what makes such material so important. Yet, as we have noted with the two cases above, this *ambiguity illusion* can be just as persuasive on film as in real life.

However, remember that 99 per cent of our evidence for monsters comes from witnesses who are employing nothing other than their demonstrably fallible human perception systems. Given that caution, we have to realize that what seems to constitute impressive corroborative support for a monster is not actually proof of any absolute reality. Simply because year after year people report seeing the same sort of thing is nothing but proof of a sort of social or psychological reality. That may or may not be the same thing as absolute reality.

Returning to the hard evidence of Loch Ness, what else does it have to offer? Two other sets of photographs are well worth considering for important reasons. There is the case of Frank Searle, former paratrooper and wanderlust adventurer, who effectively camped out by the Loch for over 15 years before setting off to roam Britain with no forwarding address and (to my latest knowledge) effectively disappearing from sight.

Searle has exacted the wrath of almost every other monster hunter. I met Roy Mackal in the USA. As a Chicago scientist, and probably the leading naturalist exponent of cryptozoology in the world, Dr Mackal has spent a great deal of time at the Loch, amongst his many other expeditions. I took his views on the monster very seriously and he was scathing about Searle, dismissing him as a scoundrel and his several photographs as fakes.

Campbell, in his book, pulls no punches, insisting on that matter that 'he resorted to photographing models and logs which he presented as pictures of N . . . Searle is now totally discredited.'

Perhaps so, but Peter Hough, with whom I have worked very closely for many years, has been a personal friend of Searle and knew the man better than almost anyone. Searle confided in Peter a great deal and gave vent to his feelings of dissatisfaction with the research efforts of some of the Loch Ness clan, which includes amongst its number the late Sir Peter Scott and also Nicholas Witchell, author of positive books on the subject before becoming one of BBC television's leading news anchormen.

In one of Searle's conversations with Peter Hough he lambasted some of those who promote the monster, although wisely refusing to name names. He says that these anonymous adherents 'want to turn the Loch into a money-making racket telling the public any old rubbish if it means they will part with their money . . . Most of the books I have read contain about 10 per cent fact and 90 per cent supposition . . . There has never been any serious, scientific investigation of Loch Ness, only gimmicks and publicity stunts . . .'[32]

One can understand very quickly from remarks such as these (which are typical — indeed a lot of the rest was completely unreproducible!) exactly why Mr Searle had such a negative effect upon his colleagues.

I even felt his wrath myself. The *News of the World* colour supplement did a feature on the Loch and called me for a comment about UFO sightings in the vicinity. I tried, very unsuccessfully as it turned out, to summarize the sort of embryonic ideas I am now developing more carefully in this book. As usual I had the standard five minutes of journalist time to do so. It came out in print as a suggestion that witnesses were all hallucinating Nessie into existence, which is not exactly what I meant. But Frank took it personally and told Peter Hough that I was 'a mad woman' who had no idea what I was talking about.

I think we can see from this that Frank Searle was highly committed to his work at the Loch. From all I have seen, read and heard from him I find it hard to view him as the rogue the rest of the monster movement want to paint him. It is possible that his greatest sin was taking several good photographs that purport to show humps and other features of the monster, *plus* the dastardly deed of also photographing in broad daylight some solid looking UFOs overflying the water.

These pictures are visually impressive. They may well be fakes as others contend, but I have not seen any proof of this. Maybe it is that Searle was just the right kind of person to get these spectacular and almost unprecedented results from Loch Ness, for reasons that might be more apparent later in this book. I hope Peter Hough continues to look into this case, as he has promised me he will, because we may learn a great deal from this strange man and his unusual photography.

Remarkably similar to Searle in some respects is Anthony 'Doc' Shiels, who is another travelling man, operating a Punch and Judy show. Being a professional on-the-road magician, Campbell refers to him in plainly derogatory fashion as a 'self-styled "wizard and professional psychic"'. He then proceeds to add that he finds his photographs 'likely hoaxes' although he offers limited evidence of that.

Firstly, let us look at the details of what are without doubt the most startling Nessie images so far captured.

At 4 p.m. on 21 May 1977, Doc Shiels was at Urquhart Castle on the shores of the Loch when Nessie 'popped up' briefly out of the water and he was able to take his two spectacular colour shots of the head and neck. These were in similar pose to the infamous surgeon's photo of 1933 but much more impressive. He stated afterwards that he believed his psychic powers were relevant and that through these he could have 'invoked' the appearance.

Shiels is a close friend of *Fortean Times* editor, Robert Rickard, who has frequently stated that he supports his integrity without question. I have never seen anything to call that evaluation into question. However, others find much about the case that is disturbing.

For example, Shiels quickly alleged that his pictures started to do disappearing acts in the post and all bar a poor copy of one of the two was lost forever under these bizarre circumstances.[33] Adding that such 'dematerializations' are often reported in

One of the two photographs of the Loch Ness monster taken by Anthony 'Doc' Shiels in the midst of the May 1977 'UFO' wave. According to computer enhancement in the USA it exhibits suggestions of semi-transparency, in that part of the water ripples can be seen through the neck under intense examination. This could be a significant clue (*Fortean Picture Library/Anthony Shiels*).

paranormal circles convinced few (although I have to say that similar things have happened to me with important original documents).

A copy of one slide was sent to Ground Saucer Watch in Arizona, a group of electronics experts who have used 'computer enhancement' techniques to investigate photographs of UFOs.

The computer breaks down the image into electrical impulses and then reassembles them. It is possible to bring out subtleties not otherwise visible and the process, developed out of deep-space probe missions where it was the only way to obtain photographs, has successfully unmasked a number of hoax UFO cases. However, it has also had its critics with genuine grounds for complaint and even Ground Saucer Watch themselves do not profess to be completely accurate in their pronouncements.

That said, Shiels freely sent the pictures and was prepared for their verdict, which is not the action of a hoaxer. Especially not one who was very well aware of the potential consequences of the analysis methods if his submitted pictures *were* hoaxed.

A major surprise came from the analysis, when the report arrived in October 1977. The computer suggested the monster image was 'flat' and that water ripples could be seen *through* the neck as if it were transparent! In the evaluators' mind this was evidence of a hoax. Doc Shiels, staggered by the revelation, was forced to ponder alternative explanations.[34]

Attesting, I think, to his honesty Shiels has allowed any professional who requested it full access to the photographs and most have come away impressed and persuaded.

However, once again the main reasons people seem to rebel against the pictures are: first, that they are so good; second, that they have features which may not support a completely flesh and blood monster; third, Shiels himself is a strange individual with alleged psychic powers.

I rather think these factors are important clues, not reasons for automatic rejection. And our interest should blossom, not wither as it will tend to do when we learn that Sheils has also 'invoked' Morgawr — another plesiosaur-like sea monster occasionally seen off the Cornish coast. This act was carried out as part of a magic ritual with 'witches' in attendance!

It should be added that Morgawr has also generated some impressive photographs, including two taken in February 1976 by a woman who was so terrified she still wishes to remain anonymous. Quite a number of other sightings have been documented.[35]

These Morgawr pictures, taken at Rosemullion Head, are probably the most dramatic ever offered as possible proof of a water monster. They show the long neck and small head in motion and a great percentage of the body raised above the water. Indeed, we can even see the way this is sufficiently flexible to display humps, which are often all that is seen above the surface in many Nessie photographs.

Again there is little evident reason to suppose the Morgawr pictures are not genuine. Yet if Doc Shiels really was able to 'raise' this monster from the waters, and later do the same at Loch Ness (getting apparent photographic proof), it poses several major questions about the nature of lake monsters.

Our conviction that we may be dealing with a real animal takes a further blow when we realize that Doc Shiels took his Nessie photographs right in the middle of the biggest UFO wave Britain has ever seen.

I can illustrate this with some hard facts. The records of NUFON (Northern UFO Network), an organization covering just northern Britain, record on average about 10 sightings a month. May 1977 has 38 cases. Of these two-thirds were in the period between May 17 and 27, and 13 of those came during the 48-hour spell between the evenings of May 20 and 22.

For Shiels' amazing photographs of Nessie to arrive precisely at the heart of the most active phase of this unparalleled UFO activity does not suggest to me an irrelevance. It implies some sort of connection.

Recently the Shiels photographs have taken on an even more incredible complexion, thanks to yet another weird twist to the story. A friend of his had a chance encounter in a library at Cumbernauld, near Glasgow. Here a small blonde woman was browsing through a pamphlet on Loch Ness (which it was later discovered the library did not stock and so she presumably must have brought herself!). In conversation, the woman said she had taken a picture very like that in the booklet (i.e. Doc Shiels'). Shiels' friend then set up a rendezvous and the photo was exchanged. It apparently seemed as if the mysterious woman, who gave little away, was 'pleased to get rid of it'.

When Doc Shiels saw the colour slide (allegedly taken in September 1983 near Achnahannet) he immediately suspected a hoax. He thought that the woman had simply taken his picture, reversed it and put the result into a shot of the Loch as a montage. He had good reason for such suspicion. The image of Nessie, including neck, head, 'eye' and open mouth was virtually identical with that on his own photograph. If it was not a hoax based on his picture then it simply had to be the same thing filmed in both cases.

However, tests carried out by photo expert and mystery animal researcher Colin Bord showed many differences. There was no sign of trickery or montage effects and *if* it was a fake then, he said, 'the hypothetical artist would have to be a master of his craft', using an airbrush to subtly alter the basic image of the monster. Another option was computer-directed alteration to the Shiels picture.

Doc Shiels, completely bamboozled by this latest development, said that he now had to wonder if someone, somewhere was not attempting an incredibly elaborate set-up by building and manipulating a 'muppet' Nessie below the water and parading it in front of two cameras seven years apart with goodness knows what kind of motivation![36]

We must leave the subject of these photographs here. I think you will already have got my main point that apparently 'solid' evidence can create more confusion than the equally problematic eyewitness testimony.

I should briefly add that the other main method of seeking out Nessie has been the use of underwater sonar. This has progressed from single ship experiments to the amazing Operation Deepscan in October 1987, which reputedly cost £1,000,000 worth of freely donated services and brought a fantastic media circus onto the Loch. They were expecting to watch the ultimate attempt to trap the monster and prove that a plesiosaur lived on.

Long-term Loch Ness researcher, Adrian Shine, masterminded the project which deployed 20 boats with sophisticated equipment loaned by companies from Oklahoma and the UK. By sweeping the entire Loch over several days they hoped to discover whether Nessie was there. In fact results were disappointing. They did find a sunken tree stump which may well have been the 'head of the monster' filmed in a 1975 underwater experiment. Otherwise few potential targets were logged.[37]

Is this yet more evidence *against* the existence of a *real* monster?

Whilst finding an aquatic monster in a Scottish lake seems a little improbable, I suspect that most people would be somewhat more tolerant of one reputed to live in a remote part of the African Congo. Indeed, it is here where the most exciting and dramatic research into a water monster has been occurring during the eighties.

We are talking about a region with tens of thousands of square miles of almost unexplored jungle, where some of the natives are very unfriendly and even said to be cannibals, where every step could bring death at the bite of one of the many poisonous creatures, such as the deadly mamba snake, and where, not surprisingly, very few people from the civilized world have had the faith to venture.

In many respects it is the archetypal 'lost world' of Arthur Conan Doyle. It is also only a few hundred miles south east from the Gambia where the 'sea monster' washed up on shore in 1983.

For much of this century the Congo has been a legendary, hostile place. But rumours of intense fascination to cryptozoologists have emerged from there. One of the best early reports was from Captain Freiherr von Stein, who led an expedition into the Likouala region during 1913 and 1914. The trek picked up many tales from natives that a giant creature lived in the rivers and pools that formed these infested swamps, hundreds of miles from any town of note.

The beast was described as 'smooth skin, brownish-grey in colour . . . approximate size that of an elephant, or at least that of a hippopotamus. It seems to have a long, flexible neck and a single (very long) tooth (or horn).' Whilst natives had allegedly been killed by the thing, when its massive tail overturned canoes that drifted too close, it was not said to be carnivorous. In fact it reportedly fed on the molombo, a flowering liana plant that thrives on the tall riverside trees.

This failure to attribute man-eating qualities to the monster supports the veracity of the stories. They came over as sightings of a real creature, not legends to terrify unfriendly neighbours. Indeed, the von Stein expedition found tracks that could well have been caused by the animal. They certainly appeared to come from a large and unknown beast.

Professor Roy Mackal, of the Biology Department at the

University of Chicago, hot from his studies into Nessie, went to the Congo in February 1980. In and around the village of Epena he found many recent eye-witnesses.

The creatures were now more accurately described as up to 40 feet in length and with a snake-like neck of reddish-brown coloration. The beast was known by the natives as *mokele-mbembe* and several had been seen in the nearby River Bai and Lake Tele (sometimes spelt in sources as Telle). He even heard the remarkable account of how in 1959 local pygmies had trapped and killed one of the giants, cutting it up for a lengthy feeding session!

Mackal insisted: 'From the reports received we concluded that *mokele-mbembe* refers to a real animal, not a myth.' He was determined to go back and try to prove this.[38]

Between October and December 1981 the scientist was able to organize the numerous tricky negotiations with the Congolese authorities. With two other scientists, Richard Greenwell and Justin Wilkinson from the University of Arizona, he set off on the hazardous journey by plane and then in a flimsy boat across the several hundred miles inland from Brazzaville.

Some achievements of the mission were confirmation that the molombo plant was real. Analysis back in Arizona found it unlikely to be a sole source of food for any large animal but also proved the liana to be almost unchanged from the cretaceous period, over 60 million years earlier. Indeed the entire Likouala region was relatively little altered in a geological sense. This fact has great importance, for this is when the last known species of dinosaur officially died out, including the herbivorous sauropod that Mackal and others now considered the most likely source of the native stories.

However, only a few near misses befell the expedition: huge gaps through the bush, apparently caused by an enormous animal that had beaten its way past in recent days; unexplained huge splashes in the water, etc. Indeed, the team were unfortunately unable to reach Lake Tele as the native guides insisted the four-day journey on foot was too risky.[39]

Meanwhile a rift developed between some members of the 1981 expedition, which was organized by the International Society for Cryptozoology. Herman Regusters, an American adventurer, had travelled with them but split away. He *did* go with some natives to Lake Tele, the source of the most dramatic reports and just 100 miles north of the equator.

After flying a low-level survey from their Epena bound STOL (short take-off and landing aircraft), on 9 October 1981, Regusters, his psychologist wife, Congolese scientists, and some natives, tracked the best route to the lake. In his exciting report the American describes how they traversed the water-sodden forests by boat until about 40 miles from the lake, then set off through the swamp on foot. This took five days and they were often waist deep in water. Around them were panthers, snakes, killer bees and innumerable crocodiles. It was no easy passage.

Finally, reaching the lake, they surveyed it thoroughly for both flora and fauna, making interesting non-supernatural discoveries. The other mission (which did not get there) later criticized stories of monsters in the water on the basis of an estimated depth of only a few feet. But Regusters and his team said that the centre depth was around 500 feet, clearly adequate given the abundant vegetation and shoals of edible fish.

Several sightings were made on their stay during October and November. The best was on 29 October when 'every member of the scientific team, except the photographer' witnessed a long neck swimming through the lake for about five minutes, before submerging. Terrible unidentified cries — 'a low windy roar, then increasing to a deep-throated trumpeting growl' — were heard on several occasions by the team, usually followed by sounds of a large animal moving through the trees or an enormous water splash.

Unfortunately the few photographs they obtained were dim, distant and fuzzy or of only parts of what might have been a large animal. Regusters tried to explain that when they saw the creature it was for a short time and they usually had to 'get over the awe' before they could do anything at all. It is fair to say that the American scientists in the other expedition rejected this 'evidence' as totally inadequate.

However, Regusters came away convinced that what they saw was a sauropod. He says it looks not unlike a brontosaurus (the most famous of all plant-eating dinosaurs), only far smaller. He suggests an atlantosaurus, based on the geological evidence. This particular species survived in local fossil records much longer than any known dinosaur.[40]

When I met Professor Mackal in Nebraska in November 1983 he was still attempting to arrange another expedition to find the real animal he remained certain was out there. His problems in raising funds and gaining Congolese permission were made all the more urgent by some amazing news he had to share with me. Earlier that year a new expedition, from the Congo authorities itself had reached Lake Tele, where they had a close encounter with the animal and took movie film of it!

The team was led by Dr Marcellin Agnagna, from the zoological gardens in Brazzaville. He had been with Mackal on the 1981 voyage, so was considered reliable. He described what happened in early May 1983 as they camped by the lake.

It is known to have been mid afternoon (between 1 May and 3 May). One of the natives was washing in the lake when he yelled to Agnagna. The scientist was taking pictures of monkeys with the movie camera, but there was a little film left. Responding to the call he went to the lake edge, and there it was, the *mokele-mbembe*, just a few hundred feet away and plain as day.

Trembling with fright and wonder, he walked into the water, wading out towards the basking dinosaur despite fearful yells from the native that his best course of action was to run. Pointing his movie camera at the creature he let the last few minutes of film roll away, convinced he now had all the proof the world would ever need. He also knew that he was creating history.

The thing was reddish-brown, but the neck glistened black in the sun. He could see how it was stretched like a giraffe's neck so that it could reach from the water surface and eat the plants from the tree tops. The small head had crocodile-like eyes, but he could see no teeth. He estimated from the back, which was largely visible above the surface, that the creature was not as huge as some of the reports, although at 15 feet still quite large enough.

He reached within 200 feet of the monster before the water got too deep. It was moving its head and neck from side to side as if listening. But he kept it in view long after the film ran out. All told he was standing less than a hundred yards from a living fossil for over 20 minutes, he said. Then it slowly sank beneath the water, as if bored by the proceedings and having had quite enough sun for one day.

Mackal described the first-hand reports from Agnagna with calm assurance. The Congolese scientist had no doubts: 'It can be said with certainty that the animal we saw was *mokele-mbembe*, that it was quite alive . . . *mokele-mbembe* is a species of sauropod living in the Likouala swamps and rivers.'

However, there was a terrible disappointment in store for the zoologist and the world. The movie camera had been on macro setting to record the monkeys. In his excitement Agnagna had simply forgotten to reset it. The dinosaur was too far away for macro. The result was a blurred mess.

But still photos had been taken whilst Agnagna was in the water. There had been time for those on land to get prepared. Only one still camera had survived the heat and humidity of the expedition and sadly, as the Congolese man sheepishly admitted, this flopped because 'we left the lens cap on'.

Roy Mackal was still hoping to get some worthwhile results from this disaster when I met him. But this proved impossible. Agnagna had written to him, pledging a return, saying, 'it may be hard to convince people because I didn't get pictures'. He was certainly right about that.

Many sceptics argued that having been out there in those terrible conditions and failing to either see or prove anything, wishful thinking and the temptation to fabricate became too powerful to resist. Nevertheless, most of those who had been to Likouala — such as Mackal — were themselves convinced the dinosaur was real, so they judged Agnagna more kindly.

Whatever the truth, May 1983 provided the greatest ever story of the one that got away!

The following year Agnagna faced attack from other crypto-zoologists, predictably infuriated that he had left them open to rebuke by their critics. If he was being truthful, then his mistake had let a once-in-a-lifetime opportunity come to nothing. Others told him he had only seen a large snake, or turtle and mistaken it for a monster. But he stuck firmly to his story and convictions about the dinosaur.

Soon after I returned from the USA I told this story to Scotsman Bill Gibbons, an ex-army survival expert with whom I had worked on some UFO investigations. It was destined to have quite an effect, because not long afterwards a friend of his inherited some money and wanted to use it on some exciting adventure. What better, Bill proposed, than a British hunt for the *mokele-mbembe*, a venture for Queen and country to beat the world.

Bill spent eighteen months planning the expedition, soon named Operation Congo with splendid logo headed by a sauropod. He tried to involve Roy Mackal, who was helpful with advice but did not wish to go along as he was planning his own journey to the area in March 1986. Gibbons intended to go in late 1985, returning at just about the time Mackal would be arriving. As he frequently told me, this meant that the longest ever continued presence in the Congo would occur during 1986 and hopefully that would make all the difference in the hunt for *mokele-mbembe*.

Accompanying Gibbons would be Mark Rothermel, Jonathan Walls and Joe Della-Porta. All were trained survivalists rather than scientists, and that created some problems at first. The scientists who had taken missions out there were reluctant to endorse what may have seemed to them like a schoolboy adventure rather than a sober, scientific quest.

Similarly, despite vague promises of support from ITV and a national newspaper, the team struggled to obtain the best sort of photographic equipment to make the treacherous voyage worthwhile. However, a few breakthroughs were made on this score and when they persuaded Marcellin Agnagna to guide them on from Brazzaville, all seemed set fair. The zoologist said he was determined to make amends for his 1983 fiasco.

Dr Angela Milner at the British Natural History Museum also confirmed that she would cooperate: 'If you are able to film and photograph the mystery animal, then I for one would be fascinated to see the results. I would not be greatly surprised if an animal new to science were discovered in such an unexplored area. However, the chances of a dinosaur turning up are remote indeed.'[41]

Nevertheless, in a later letter, Dr Milner confirmed that the Museum would examine 'any serious and objective evidence' that Gibbons might come up with. She also helped the team plan more reserved scientific observations whilst out in this little understood environment, and indeed they did record a species of monkey not witnessed before.

Shortly before he left from Liverpool, Bill Gibbons told me in a letter: 'I am confident that, in view of our collective field experience, field strategy and length of stay in Africa we will herald concrete evidence on the existence of *mokele-mbembe*.'[42]

Gibbons was nothing if not confident. The last time I spoke to him days before he left he insisted: 'I am convinced there is a herd of these animals out there. We have carefully logged all the areas where there have been sightings . . . We are absolutely determined to bring proof back to Britain.'

He added that their fitness and jungle experience were a bonus and scotched the arguments of some cryptozoologists that they were playing at monster hunting by noting: 'We have the best of both worlds, because we are taking with us the one scientist who has *seen* the creature.'

One major scheme would be to set up stakes near the lake edge with tree-mounted cameras set to go off automatically. All they had to do was somehow persuade the creature to fall for the trap. Also they planned to train a native to use a simple polaroid camera so that they could leave this after their return home and increase the odds of gaining proof.

I pointed out how dangerous the whole thing sounded and Bill shrugged this off with the words: 'We have very good guns — and I am constantly testing mine!'

However, as it turned out the expedition went far from well. They had problems with the free ride on a freighter ship to take them to the Congo. After getting there at last on 30 December 1985 a change in the government had meant the officials who had approved their expedition were out of a job. Weeks of waiting, requesting, being forced into bribing people and held up 'on remand' with passports confiscated, put all their plans in jeopardy as the money began to run out.

Back in Britain the magazine *Fortean Times* sold dinosaur T-shirts to try to raise funds to keep the mission alive. But when £1000 was sent from London it ended up as just £100 after passage through the Congolese banking 'system'.

When they eventually did get out into Likouala, weeks late, they say that Agnagna was more of a hindrance than a help. According to Bill Gibbons, in June 1986, the scientist had kept referring to them as 'children' and 'weaklings' and constantly ridiculed their efforts. Once he urged the natives to leave them in the bush to find their own way to the lake. Then he held onto equipment they claimed to have only loaned to him. The team were befriended by a local pastor who arranged for them to see a judge and the matter was resolved. But Agnagna quit the expedition and went home to Brazzaville.

Some days were spent at Lake Tele and they interviewed eye witnesses of the creature. They saw some tree damage and six-inch footprints consistent with reports, but no actual sign of the monster itself. Great fear of the animal was displayed by the natives who wanted to charge astronomical fees to guide them to its home. Quite what hand Agnagna had in all this is unclear. He refused to show them the location where his aborted photography allegedly happened, remarking that the team were 'too ignorant to question me'. He later wrote to Richard Greenwell, the American scientist who went with Mackal in 1981. In this report he made clear that he had acted as he did because he felt the British expedition a farce. He said that he had deliberately steered Operation Congo away from the most likely locations where *mokele-mbembe* might be, because 'these English children were very ignorant and they did not even know why they had come to the Congo'.[43]

What Marcellin Agnagna's reported behaviour has to say about his unfortunate photographic flop in 1983 — if it says anything at all — is best left up to the reader to judge.

Roy Mackal's 1986 expedition was aborted through lack of money and the continuing political problems. Possibly the Congolese prefer to keep the story of the monster alive, rather than have the matter settled one way or another. But there are several people itching to get back out there and one day soon the truth about this living lake monster might be revealed.

And so we face the key question: are any of these water monsters real? This is an interesting problem which is far from easy to decide upon. Certainly we saw from our studies that there are major difficulties hanging over some of the cases.

Personally, I would not rule out the existence of a surviving dinosaur in Lake Tele. Even the Natural History Museum seem willing to consider it, and the environment there is just about right. Of course, if *mokele-mbembe* is more than a myth then it has to leave the way open for other lakes to possess distant cousins. Of all the monsters in this book, the most likely candidate to exist in flesh and blood reality is this consistently-reported descendant of the dinosaur, although it must have evolved in some ways since the cretaceous period and may not be exactly like the sauropods of old.

Having said that I think we cannot run away from the fact that in most of the cases we have examined there were psychological factors to the fore which were as important as any physical considerations. As we saw at Loch Ness, even the best of hard evidence raises questions about what level of reality we should expect the monster to occupy.

I think it appropriate to leave the last word to Michel Meurger, a French researcher. Discussing the innumerable sightings of a beast in the Canadian lakes he points out that no one animal seems to fit all the stories. But surely there cannot be several dinosaur species? This would indeed pose a problem if the animal behind the stories were real. So he tends to feel otherwise and has even coined the term 'mythozoologist' for researchers into these subjects.

He adds: 'My fieldwork in Quebec seems to indicate that it would be more promising to study the inhabitants on the shores of a lake than to probe its murky waters.'[44]

There is unquestionably much truth in that suggestion.

3.

Earth Monsters

When organized searches are made, the animals are strangely
elusive and can rarely be found and never caught.

Janet and Colin Bord,
leading cryptozoologists and photographers

Flatwoods, West Virginia, sounds like the perfect movie-
inspired 'hick' town from the southern United States. But on 12
September 1952 it generated a very scary monster tale.

As the sun went down behind a local hill a group of youths
reported a 'meteor' trailing red sparks out of the sky. Scurrying
up to investigate, like youngsters the world over might do, they
say that a nightmare awaited them.

Lest you start to think stray thoughts about imaginative, storytelling children, bored and with nothing else to do, or should
you see the interesting similarity with science-fiction movies
where a meteor introduces a monster to some back-of-beyond
town, then bear something else in mind.

On the way to their exploration they stopped to pick up one
of their friend's mothers, Kathleen May, and she brought with
her both her sons *and* Gene Lemon, who was a national
guardsman.

Beyond the crest of the hill an orb of light was glowing. The
moon perhaps? I have certainly known very similar cases
where, incredible as it may seem, that *was* precisely what the
mistaken witnesses were looking at. Its illusionary gigantic size
as it rises through low cloud can be confusing.

No matter: the intrepid voyagers continued up the rise, straining their ears in the gloom and hinting they could hear 'hissing' or 'throbbing' noises (they did not agree amongst themselves and some heard nothing at all).

Also, the hill was covered in a peculiar fog, or mist from which was pouring out a sickly, pungent odour which was making their eyes water. One youth even briefly passed out and a dog, which had run up alongside them, was barking and had its hackles up. Eventually, yelping madly, it fled off back towards the town.

Then, in the flickering light of a flashlamp, orange glowing eyes appeared, peering out angrily from a strangely oval face with a weird pointed chin. A monstrous semi-human form was in front of them, at least ten feet tall (although they only saw the top of it as the lower part was hidden by trees and shadow). It was also heading straight at them!

The assembled meteor hunters made a rapid exit down the slope, certain that they saw the figure *float* or *fly* after them. Several were violently ill with the shock, which the local news-paperman, who had interviewed them right away, was convinced indicated their total sincerity. The sheriff organized a posse and scoured the top of the hill with guns trained on every treetop. Traces of the odour remained, but only some 'skid' marks, inevitably tied in by the witnesses with what they saw, provided physical evidence.

Perhaps these people were entirely credible; although the investigating US Air Force (who considered this case their province!) concluded the story was nothing but exaggeration based on a woodland animal!

It is interesting that the 'Flatwoods Monsters' became rapidly associated with UFOs, for little reason save the original report of the 'meteor' (which very likely *was* precisely that and completely unrelated). Also, of course, because of our modern cultural desire to pigeonhole phenomena, we like to relate strange phenomena with spacemen.[45]

We have many other cases of 'flying' people. Sometimes they are linked with what may be called UFOs, as for instance, the sighting in September 1954 published by the Lincoln, Nebraska, *Star,* which referred to a farmer's son in Coldwater, Kansas, who was trundling along on the tractor when a small humanoid figure with long ears literally floated overhead and disappeared in the general direction of a hill (note the frequency of this motif, by the way!). Behind the rise was a small disc into which the three- or four-foot tall entity levitated himself and departed skyward.

Identical stories are known the world over. For instance, there is a classic tale which took place in broad daylight on 29 August 1967 on (guess what?) a 'small hill' near Cussac in France. Here two children, Francois and Anne-Marie Delpeuch, were looking after the family cows with the farm dog when a group of four or five 'young children' were seen surrounding a strange grounded sphere. Thinking they had come to 'play' the youngsters approached, only to discover that these were not human children at all. Indeed, they described them as 'devils', about three and a half feet tall, with large heads, pointed chins and black and hairy silhouettes.

The figures were floating or flying upwards, turning on their heads and entering the silvery sphere in this most ungainly and amazing manner.

With the cows now lowing and heading towards the sphere and the dog yapping and prepared to give pursuit, the sphere circled in the air as it rose upwards and drifted away. Only a faint whistle and pungent smell like sulphur wafted through the air as it trailed away. The children, now terrified and crying, fled home in tears.

Excellent and immediate follow-up by investigators Joel Mesnard and Claude Pavy revealed nothing to question the truthfulness of these witnesses. They also made the interesting point that it is not difficult to mistake ozone emissions for sulphur if concentration is sufficient. The suggestion was that the sphere was ionizing the air to create this ozone — a common feature in such stories.[46]

Of course, flying humans would not be found outside such rural communities in foreign climes, would they? Well, yes, in fact they would.

Stephen Banks and Martin Keatman, two British researchers, compiled a report for the national archives in 1981 on a case that took place in Baddeley Green, Staffordshire. But again there are major similarities — most notably that the witness is once again a very young child (aged eight on this occasion).

The sighting took place in the autumn of 1976 around 9.30 p.m. The boy was awoken by a faint humming sound and was so intrigued he clambered on top of the storage heater to peer out of his bedroom window. Drifting at little more than walking pace were two small men, about four feet tall, and dressed in an all-in-one white suit ('like baby's wear' the youngster graphically and convincingly described it). Dark visors masked their faces.

But by far the most unusual feature was that they were flying, in a swimming posture, but without moving arms or legs. He saw them perfectly, illuminated by the streetlamps, and insisted they passed by within just a few feet of him. On their backs were white 'boxes'.

We may be tempted to dismiss this account, but it is so similar to all the others that we get an eerie feeling of childish innocence, which far from providing less credible evidence seems to afford absolutely *reliable* data.

Certainly Banks and Keatman were persuaded. They noticed how the boy did not call the creatures aliens, or spacemen (as he had no reason to do, of course). Instead he referred to the figures as 'masters' (local dialect for adults). He also gave further indication of his sincerity by asking the investigators several times 'who were these masters?'[47]

Incidentally, lest you think the pattern was broken in Staffordshire, it was not. Baddeley Green is surrounded by the southern rim of the Pennine Hills. And, if the West Virginia creature was floating above the ground (remember its lower half was not seen) then its height may well have been considerably less than that estimated based on the assumption that it was standing on the ground. It too might have been just four feet tall.

We are building up an interesting pattern of features that are consistent from case to case. One we have already noted is the stress often placed on the creature's eyes. This crops up again in a chilling case reported to me direct by a witness, whom I shall just call Ken. He now serves as an ambulance crew member in Cheshire, but was at the time a non-commissioned officer in the army.

The date was September 1968 and the place the main British barracks on the mountainous island of Cyprus, tucked in strategically off the coasts of the volatile Middle Eastern nations which were at the time undergoing one of their heightened states of tension.

The building had two wings and spread out onto two storeys. Ken had the responsibility of looking after the left-wing upper floor and because of this had a private billet facing the stairwell that led down to the other floor.

He was asleep, but beside him in the room was his Turkish wolfhound, a particularly large and fierce animal that served as the perfect guard dog. As Ken said: 'He was literally afraid of nothing.'

Something had evidently disturbed the dog and his growls quickly brought Ken around. He saw that it was just after 3 a.m. Instantly shaking himself alert, Ken's thoughts switched to recent terrorist activity and it took but a moment to perceive his duty.

He called out to the dog, but the animal simply refused to respond to its name. Its fur was 'as high as I have ever seen it'. The failure of the dog to calm at his touch was unprecedented, as was its evident and alarming increase in fear. It was positively reacting to something beyond the threshold of the army officer's perception and was now 'crying and shaking and then it crawled under my bed'.

Only at this point in the proceedings did Ken's attention switch away from the animal to what might be causing its distress. He picked up a faint high-pitched noise and says: 'It was acute and really penetrated the ears.' Dogs are capable of hearing sounds well above the normal range of humans (hence the use of ultrasonic whistles which are inaudible to humans but are piercingly audible to dogs). All of which suggests that the noise which Ken was detecting had an even more intense quality at a frequency beyond about 18,000 Hertz. Presumably the dog was attempting to get away from it by hiding underneath the bed.

So Ken opened the door to ascertain where the noise was coming from. He was prepared for possible saboteurs, but not for what he confronted instead: 'To my horror I saw something coming up the stairs. The description which follows is exact with no detail left out and no fabrications . . .'

The thing was just coming into view half way up the steps with its head visible through the bars that lined the stairwell.

'Its head was covered in red hair which was rough and about four inches long and stuck out in all directions. As it came higher and more came into view it became obvious that it wasn't moving normally, i.e. not taking the steps but apparently *floating* up. By this time all the head and neck was in full view and the head started to rotate towards me. The movement was completely unnatural, because the head turned too far and stayed perfectly level. The chin came right round past the left shoulder!'

Seeing the apparition head on added new frightening detail. The face was 'flat' and orange. Immediately noticeable were 'the eyes — they were looking directly at me and were very large . . . and very red.'

Ken just had time to take in the fact that the entity seemed to be wearing light blue jumpsuit-type clothing, when he decided to shut the door in absolute panic. The high-pitched note was now very intense and his teeth were vibrating, although whether from the noise or terror it was hard to tell.

He bolted the door and leapt back. The dog was still under the bed, shaking and whimpering as if having an uncontrollable fit. Ken was not too far behind him on that score. He says: 'I sat on my bed facing the door and was in very deep shock, shaking so much that my joints felt as if they were clattering about and my feet kept leaving the floor. I then became aware of a sliding sound approaching the door . . .'

Mad with fear, Ken did an instinctive roll to one side and picked up his spear gun which he used for underwater fishing in the clear blue waters. Being a well-trained soldier he never leaves such a weapon loaded indoors and the strength required is such that it normally has to be wedged against a rock and the bolt forced home. However, the incredible surge of adrenalin that fear can bring enabled him to take the gun in one hand and the spear in another and ram it home in a moment. Indeed, he even exceeded the normal limit he could force the tension back.

Not content with even this protection, the trained man grabbed his diver's knife and clutched it tight. He sat 'facing the door and feeling completely helpless' with both the knife and speargun ready to slice through the monster if it dared to open the door.

The seconds dragged on. Ken had to fight the urge to release the gun, knowing that its spear would glide through the wood as if it were made of paper. He adds that in the aftermath the things he found most surprising were that he had the composure to prevent himself from firing blindly and also that he was continually rationalizing and questioning 'what *is* that thing?'

He heard the sliding noises move past, seem to return, but keep on going, becoming fainter and fainter. The high-pitched noise departed with them. He collapsed in a heap onto the bed and was still prone in that position an hour later when one of the guards arrived to give him his early morning call.

Ken asked the guard, without saying why he was doing so, if he had seen or heard anything strange. The guard shook his head, puzzled, and looked at Ken oddly. He was baffled by the officer having his knife and speargun by his side, which seemed to be taking security precautions to the limit. But as Ken knew only too well, having these things in front of him was all the proof he needed that the experience had not been a dream. He also realized how lucky he was that he did not fire the gun through the door, because then he would have had no choice but to try and explain why he took such action. And who on earth would believe such a ludicrous truth?

As for the wolfhound, Ken says it never recovered. Afterwards it was useless as a guard dog; it would throw its legs into the air and roll over in a sign of total submission at the slightest threat.

Whilst we can have no idea what this entity was that floated into the barracks that night, I think Ken's description of the terror that both he and the animal faced up to is the most persuasive I have ever come across. It is difficult to imagine somebody inventing such raw fear, especially a soldier who might be expected to want to impress you with his bravery. Yet, isn't this exactly what *would* happen if we were to come face to face with the inexplicable?

I do not think it is accidental that many of these stories were reported in a UFO context: that just happens to be the appropriate modern scenario. However, what is much more apparent when we study cases of earthly monsters, like these or 'bigfoot', is that the distinctions and dividing lines that separate them from other phenomena are by no means clear cut. In fact we learn a lot more from the overlaps than we do from treating them as special or unique.

All over the world there are reports of creatures on the shadowy edge between ape and man. They go by many names: the Indian term *sasquatch* (demonstrating their antiquity in North American tradition) or the more evocative *bigfoot*. In the Far East they are more commonly known as the *yeti* or abominable snowman, and there are plenty of other terms as well from the remote and not so remote quarters said to be inhabited by these creatures.

Common mythology places them as some sort of throwback to Neanderthal Man, perhaps even the infamous 'missing link' said to form the bridge between the pre-hominid apes and first primitive version of *homo sapiens*. Of course, why such an entity should survive, when early species from which man has evolved died out millions or tens or thousands of years ago, is the typical question we face, as is the apparently widespread nature of these animals which leaves us pondering just how proof has been avoided all these years.

Bigfoot reports come from many American states, notably the ones with mountainous areas covered in forest such as California or Oregon. However, a rather unusual state to generate quite a plethora is the generally flat ranchland of Nebraska.

Ray Boeche has collated a number of sightings and one in particular is worth noting. It happened in August 1976 on a farm near Lincoln, one of Nebraska's principal towns.

It was dusk and a woman was on her porch looking to the south-west when she noticed that her horses were reacting to something in a restless manner. At the same time, she says, all the sounds of wildlife suddenly went still. This mysterious silence that descends over an area in the moments before a paranormal event is in fact remarkably common. We find it in UFO close encounters, psychic visions and many other episodes. I use the term 'Oz factor' to describe it, and believe that it suggests a sort of inner tuning, as the percipient's mind blocks out attention to all external sounds in order to note the message that is about to bombard his or her consciousness.

Meanwhile, back on the ranch, the woman in Nebraska now saw a figure silhouetted against the darkening sky. She was certain it was a tall human-like ape which began to run across the land towards her. At this instant her dogs scrambled up, literally bowled her over and made a desperate attempt to escape into the house.

The creature ran through a fence, across the road and then simply vanished. She is adamant that she did not lose it. The entity *disappeared*. The rancher found some hair samples on the fence which she believed to come from the monster, but she could not get any local officials to take them away for analysis. [48]

We find the same sort of pattern wherever we look at these 'man beasts'.

In Australia they go by the name of the *yowie*. According to Janet and Colin Bord, who have studied the cases in detail, most reports concentrate on the spectacular Blue Mountains of New South Wales. But they also occur on the Gold Coast of Queensland.

A typical case from here was investigated by Rex Gilroy, the Australian cryptozoologist. It took place at Springbrook on 29 January 1978, when the creature, jet black with very prominent eyes and six feet tall, was curious enough to look inside a house. The startled witness threw a chair at the thing and it 'limped' away. He said it smelt like a 'badly-kept public lavatory'. Again we see the consistent features of bad odours and unusually noticeable eyes.

The *yeti* is the equivalent creature reported most often from the Himalayas on the Tibet/Nepal/India borders. Sometimes said to be white and depicted as such in most presentations (i.e. white to camouflage it against the snow is the popular impression) in fact most reliable sightings speak of a figure that is almost identical with bigfoot or sasquatch and normally dark in colour.

Because these mountainous, snowy regions are very sparsely inhabited and contain the highest and harshest peaks on earth, they produce very sporadic sightings. Often these come from mountaineering expeditions.

A typical report is that of the Italian climber Reinhold Messner who says he was only feet away from a yeti in July 1986. He was at nearly 14,000 feet in the Tibetan Himalayas when a creature appeared from behind a tree.

His first thought was that it was a yak, but he soon realized his mistake. He was adamant that it was not 'a man nor an ape nor a bear' — which, if true, pretty well rules out the normal options in these parts.

He describes the thing as over six feet tall with shaggy black hair (but less on the face). After standing on two legs it ran off on all fours — behaviour akin to a bear but very unusual for these sort of stories. Still Messner was in no doubt and said he would go back and obtain proof.[49]

However, sightings of yeti are much rarer than sightings of their alleged footprints. Because of the abundant snow these are far more obvious than bigfoot tracks might be if left in the middle of a North American forest. Also, if you are on a remote mountain miles from any help and you come across strange tracks stretching towards the horizon, your mind may easily turn to what manner of beast has caused them.

The 1951 Mount Everest mission photographed some spectacular footprints of this sort and Eric Shipton provided an excellent close up of one print for the Royal Geographic Society. Measured against his ice axe you can see the typical wide form, with three toes, and in length at least one and a half times that of an adult human foot.

However, one thing which has to be remembered is the effect of sunlight on snow. It melts things. Prints that are not fresh could look strange because they have partially thawed and so 'spread out' to a larger size. (This is very easy to observe with your own footprints on a snowy day. After a few hours in the sun they seem to grow larger.)

This effect on potential yeti prints was reported first-hand by a Cheshire man, Anthony Wooldridge, who had the fortune to take what he considers may be the first photographs not just of yeti footprints, but of the creature itself.

On 6 March 1986 this electricity worker was on a sponsored run, earning money for charity by racing through miles of the Indian Himalayas all alone. The hazardous adventure was half-way complete when, on this particular date, he was due to climb several thousand feet up the valley towards Hemkund, crossing a desolate mountain face with no habitation.

Near 10,000 feet in late morning he came upon an area where he was convinced the snow had been recently disturbed by some animal. A small set of unusual tracks curved in an arc and then back into the trees. He paused to take some quick photographs before continuing, as time was critical to his journey. But half an hour later, upon just coming into barren mountainside above the tree-line, he heard a rumbling and stopped. There was clearly an avalanche nearby.

Across his path now lay the debris of a snow slide, which meant that he had to abandon his plans of continuing on to Hemkund and think about returning. But he was mesmerized by the strange creature standing by a shrub on the far side of the avalanche path. It was erect, with legs sunk into the snow, but probably at least six feet tall. It appeared man-like but was covered in dark hair. He knew that the only creature which would fit the facts was the yeti, even though he had been completely sceptical about its existence until that moment.

Wooldridge got as close as he could without risking entry onto the open avalanche path. This meant he was never less than several hundred feet away. But in compensation he took some photographs from slightly different vantage points. However, during the 45 minutes that he remained watching and taking pictures, the yeti was virtually immobile. Its incredible ability to stand upright, effectively imitating a rock, surprised him. But there was little question it *was* animate and the photographs appear to vindicate his opinion.

On his way back he saw many other tracks in the snow and when he passed the ones he had photographed three hours before he filmed them again. They had deteriorated appreciably in the interim.

Anthony Wooldridge made no attempt to use his photographs to publicize his fund-raising. Indeed, he did all the publicity for this on return without even mentioning what he had captured with his small Nikon camera. He had decided not to precipitate a hunt for the yeti by generating hysterical reaction and instead allowed first the BBC *Wildlife* magazine and then the cryptozoological press to have his story, rather than the tabloids.[50]

I think this attitude and responsible concern speaks volumes for his sincerity.

Needless to say quite a controversy broke out over his evidence, but the majority of naturalists could come up with no plausible answer to what else might have been standing beside the mountain slope. Even the sceptical anthropologist,

Professor Robert Martin of University College, London, told the BBC that there was: 'a marginal possibility that a large-bodied primate as yet undocumented by zoologists inhabits the Himalayas'. In other words, it *might* be a yeti![51] However, in 1989 a further expedition and new photographic analysis has revealed that the monster was almost certainly an oddly-shaped rock. It seems that we must now accept that expectation (based on the still unexplained footprints) and strangeness of environment can play quite a part in generating 'pseudo-monsters'. An important lesson.

Even better film exists of the bigfoot variety — always presuming any of it is genuine. Roger Patterson and Bob Gimlin took motion pictures of a large black creature emerging from woods at Bluff Creek, California, on 20 October 1967. If it is real then it allegedly shows a beast measured at 6 feet 8 inches tall and over 400 pounds. Nevertheless, it is virtually impossible to distinguish between a real man-ape and a sophisticated monkey suit and suspicions are aroused by its rather human-like gait.

Interestingly there was a major UFO sighting wave during that precise week in October 1967. In Britain it was the largest wave to occur before the May 1977 series, and coincided exactly with the Nessie images. It this relevant?

Other film of bigfoot is even more dramatic, but has problems. Taken by hunter Ivan Marx, it reputedly shows a sasquatch charging out of bush and straight at him. This was near Mount Lassen, California. He promptly aimed his rifle and shot the black monster. Our credibility threshold becomes tested when we learn that he kept the camera running to see the thing stumble away into the trees. It was then able to 'get up, after tumbling end over end, agonizing and convulsing'.

Nor does it help to learn that Marx has seen and filmed the creature on other occasions and that all of this evidence is currently available for around $40, if you send for the movie he distributes from his footage, entitled *In the Shadows of Bigfoot*.[52] Perhaps this is genuine and Marx was just very lucky, but the sceptics are understandably suspicious.

The sporadic nature of this hard evidence for the man-apes clashes with those cases which are truly extraordinary — *paranormal*, in fact. We saw the example of the vanishing bigfoot in Nebraska and these supernatural trappings are quite commonplace.

A very good case was investigated first hand by Jerome Clark and Loren Coleman at Roachdale, Indiana, in August 1972. Randy and Lou Rogers moved into a farmhouse with their family and mysterious attacks began on their chickens. Often this seemed to be gratuitous slaughter with the mutilated birds not being eaten, but left in a mass of blood and gore.

The cause was seen on a number of occasions, silhouetted against the barn door or in the road. It seemed to be a large ape like a gorilla and there were indications that something had flattened bushes. However, when fired upon at point-blank range the creature was neither felled nor wounded. It seemed as if the bullets went *straight through it*, bemused witnesses insisted.

Local lawmen and a conservation officer, William Woodall, arrived on the scene. Most saw the creature, but as Woodall later said: 'I never could find any concrete physical evidence.'

Mrs Rogers was even more explicit about the strange nature of this bigfoot: 'We would never find tracks, even when it ran over mud. It would run and jump but it was like it wasn't touching anything. And sometimes when you looked at it, it looked like you could see *through* it.'[53]

Again local UFO sightings had a part in the story. But whether they were directly connected never became clear. However, there are plenty of cases where the interrelationship is apparent.

Don Worley is one of America's leading researchers into the UFO and bigfoot mysteries and has amply demonstrated that correlation. He kindly kept me in touch with his work via interview tapes and other material.

He describes a significant case from north-eastern Ohio, involving Ben — a Vietnam war veteran who observed lights and then a 'banana boat'-shaped object in broad daylight hovering above his farm during the early part of 1981.

But this was just the start of a terrifying experience which developed during May and June as animals began to be attacked with claws, and his ducks all ended up with their heads bitten off.

Now alerted, Ben responded to the slightest noise outside and one night caught a strange creature in his flashlight beam. It was 'a big black form with two red glowing eyes'. Later he was able to measure it against a winch and it was over *nine* feet tall!

Ben fired a shot and scared it away. But it returned next night, when he caught his dog 'barking uncontrollably' then making 'a loud whimpering cry' and 'frantically trying to dig itself a space under the lawnmower'; all of which sounds very similar to what befell the wolfhound in the Cyprus army barracks and suggests a fearful response to some extrasensory input.

As the siege went on, many lights were seen dancing over the woods, projecting beams to the ground and with the red eyes of the man-apes wandering in the bush beneath. Also 'transmogrifications' took place, with human-like shapes emerging out of the shadowed forms and growing from what were at first just bluish/white lights.

We might be tempted to wonder if Ben and his family were reading shapes into ordinary lights, but this emergence of strange patterns from out of what were basically just glowing lights (in a coal-mining state laced with fault lines) is something to store away for later recollection.

Ben also noted that his teenage son, Andy, acted like a catalyst. When the lights were at their peak the boy would 'lapse into a sleep-like state from which he could not be awakened'. He always 'came to' when taken to relatives but with no memory as to what had taken place. Read any book about UFO abductions and you will find this 'time lapse' repeated again and again. Andy also said 'teachers' came into his bedroom at night.[54]

One major clue is that these victims only attempted one photograph of an ape figure. Despite its clear appearance to the naked eye, the developed photograph showed just 'a softball-sized glowing ball with fluorescent red/orange streaks'. Eventually the sad affair ended when the family split up.[55]

This attempt at photography may be highly significant. It surely suggests that what the camera recorded (the fuzzy light) is what was actually present. In other words, the rest of the sighting was presumably grafted onto the blob somewhere within the perception systems of the human witnesses. This monster truly was a *mind* monster.

Let us progress further down a parallel track by looking at a monster that is far more widespread than bigfoot. We would be most unlikely to meet up with a sasquatch down the local high street, but the chances of crossing the path of a 'phantom feline' are much greater.

Of course big cats, such as lynxes, panthers or pumas are native to some countries, including remoter parts of the USA. But there are none in Britain. The only form that comes even close is the Scottish mountain 'wild cat' which, although a different variety altogether, looks not unlike a rather ferocious version of the fireside tabby. However, this does not even begin to compare in size or description with the slinky dark coat and considerable bulk of the big cats, familiar to most of us only from wildlife parks or zoos.

It does not seem easy to imagine that people would mistake a 'wild cat' for a 'big cat', especially when the sightings are not in the highlands but in suburbia.

Yet sightings happen with surprising frequency. Janet and Colin Bord document the extraordinary hunt for the 'Surrey

Worplesdon, Surrey, just north-west of Guildford, is an area where UFO activity has been intense. It is also within the zone of main activity of the 'Surrey puma' in the early sixties. Two former police photographers captured this shot of an unexplained large cat on 14 August 1966 and, despite various suggestions that it merely shows a feral (or wild domestic) cat, the witnesses suspect otherwise (*Fortean Picture Library*).

puma' between 1962 and 1965, when so many reports flooded into police from the London stockbroker belt and local farm animals were butchered. There was little doubt in most inhabitants' minds that a real big cat (or several of them) was on the loose. Huge searches and heavily-armed police hunts took place, because it was feared the creature might be a danger to children. But absolutely no concrete proof of the animal ever materialized.[56]

In 1966 two former police photographers succeeded in getting a close range shot of the 'puma' near Worplesdon. However, the beast that is looking straight at the camera resembles a smaller and more mundane cat, even though the witnesses were insistent it was not.

Other ideas ranged from misperceptions of renegade dogs (certain thin breeds like labradors can look not unlike big cats from a distance), to the most common explanation, that the cats were merely true exotic species kept by eccentric people as pets and which had escaped from their owners, or had run away from private zoos or circuses. Because many of these would not be easy to trace (would you report losing a panther if you kept one without a licence?) this explanation could account for a *few* cases, but not for so many reports.

If the sightings had been confined to Surrey then the 'escapee' solution might seem appropriate. There have probably been occasions where this certainly does apply. For instance, I live in a district of Stockport, Cheshire, that can hardly be classified as rural. So I can well imagine the surprise of Margaret O'Malley, who lives about a mile from me in Adswood, when she left the house for work one morning in May 1983. On the roof of her garden shed was a puma. This was no mistake or hallucination, unless hallucinations are capable of drinking saucers of milk. The shy animal was promptly rounded up by a girl on horseback, who trotted down the street and explained that the cat had escaped from a travelling circus. Meanwhile police surrounded the house in the mistaken impression that this council estate was under siege from a ferocious wild animal.

However, big cats have been seen all over Britain on far too many occasions for all of them to be runaways from the local fair. There are also interesting little clues that link them in with the paranormal.

For instance, what is one to think of the hunt for the cat that
stalked farms in Scotland in late 1977 and early 1978, during a
UFO flap? It made its home at Bettyhill — which, as any student
of UFO lore will tell you, brings a smile to the lips. (The first
woman to claim abduction by a UFO in public was an
American about whom a bestselling book and movie were
produced. Her name was Betty Hill.)[57]

As the years rolled by the cases poured in from many diverse
sources. The term 'puma' was frequently used, even though the
animal described was often black and much more like a
panther.

In Kent in 1979 police hunted the creature. Chief Inspector
Carey was quoted as saying that there were too many sensible
reports for them to be dismissed. But the police never caught
it. Plaster casts taken of some prints possibly left behind could
not be identified by Canterbury Zoo. London Zoo were much
more forthcoming, insisting the prints were not made by any
recognizable cat and were probably made by a dog. Therefore,
the police concluded, the panic was over. The phantom *was* a
dog. Of course, those who had seen it and were convinced
otherwise became infuriated by this rejection of their testimony.

Perhaps the most widely publicized big-cat hunt took place
on Exmoor in Devon during the summer of 1983. This is the
area where Sherlock Holmes chased the 'Hound of the Basker-
villes', a powerful myth in the local subconscious that might well
be relevant. Certainly, after a trickle of reports of a large black
cat and many mysterious sheep deaths the rumours grew into
legendary proportions.

The police constantly tried to play down the stories, alleging
the animal was merely a big dog, and eventually a greyhound
cross-breed. Witnesses were insistent that it was far too big, and
when big cats clock in at around six to eight feet long and three
feet high then it is hard to see how anything but a most extraordinary dog could be misperceived.

Another factor was that the sheep were killed in a particularly
vicious manner: their heads were crushed and the body fluids
sucked out. Whatever was causing the hysteria it was soon
obvious that the animal needed to be caught. National papers
put up rewards for photographs and carcasses. Farmers started
to patrol nervously with rifles and Di Francis, who was

researching the stories in total conviction that a strain of big cats *was* living wild throughout Britain, joined in a sort of 'save the pussy' campaign.[58]

Going out on patrol with the marines she spent days on the moors between April and August looking for proof. As usual it never arrived, although the killings went on. Rather half-heartedly the soldiers spoke of the culprit being our old friend a dog. But it was certainly elusive, and as with all other stories from the length and breadth of Britain, dog or cat the creature was remarkably able to evade a 'manhunt' that few cunning humans could have escaped.[59]

Michael Goss, one of our best researchers into strange lifeforms, personally investigated another spate of reports from Essex just a few months later.

They centred on 4 November 1983 at Horndon-on-the-Hill, just north of the Thames estuary. Mrs Anne Cheale of Great Malgraves Farm had the best view whilst sitting with a friend and with her Dobermans lounging nearby. The animal was in the grass several hundred feet away, but she watched it through binoculars for some time until it was seen to get up and then move away. She described it as the size of a Doberman but 'all black' and 'definitely a cat' with a 'low slung body'. She said that even though such a conclusion was 'illogical' her eyesight clearly demonstrated the animal was a panther. Her conviction was absolute that it was somebody's escaped pet.

Local police had other reports, but they never found the culprit of course. They concluded it was a dog, but Mrs Cheale, as a farmer, was very familiar with animal life, owned her own large dogs and noted how both of these had become 'aware' of the creature, or of her response to it.

All over Britain the story is the same. Andy Roberts provides a nice survey of some of the sightings in the north in his appropriately titled little booklet *Cat Flaps.*[60]

He notes cases from Lancashire, Yorkshire, Cheshire, Derbyshire and Nottinghamshire. In every one of these flaps there were repeated sightings. The animals were variously termed 'lions', 'cougars', 'lynxes' and 'panthers'; although it is unlikely that any of these names are more accurate than convenient labels adopted by the media.

All the familiar features turned up in these different waves.

The Harrogate 'panther' in the autumn of 1985 scared dogs, had glowing eyes, left no evidence and was never caught. Naturalists stated it was probably just a feral cat (a large domestic cat, living wild).

In the Rossendale Valley of Lancashire, the 'Beast of Bacup' (usually interpreted as a lion) was seen the previous summer. Even the local police warned people to stay off the moors and there were mysterious sheep killings which convinced the villagers that the animal was living in disused quarries. Yet, it is fascinating to note that these quarries at Stacksteads (the small settlement where I was born) have spawned one of the biggest UFO hotspots in Britain today, ever since October 1978 when a disc of light was seen to 'land' there.

One of the most impressive cases occurred in November 1980 at Todmorden, about five miles east. A police officer had a close encounter whilst on duty. Under hypnosis he later 'recalled' an abduction on board a UFO. He says that a large black animal was inside the UFO with him. He called it a 'dog', but as we have seen before there is often considerable uncertainty about the dog/cat description. [61]

Indeed local legends all over Britain are full of stories of what are usually called 'black dogs'. These are described as having by now very familiar features: glowing eyes, a pungent odour, and the ability to vanish into thin air.

The most famous example comes from Blythburgh church in Suffolk, where a black dog allegedly manifested during the middle of an electrical storm on 4 August 1577. What can be taken as scorch marks from the paws are still visible on the door.

Blythburgh lies about ten miles north of the Leiston/ Rendlesham Forest area and eight miles north of Sizewell. The forest was host to Britain's most astonishing UFO sighting in December 1980, when something reputedly crashed into trees and left radiation behind. [62] Sizewell is the home of the highly controversial nuclear reactors. Both Blythburgh and Sizewell generated impressive close encounter cases in February 1975, typical of many in the vicinity investigated by the late Peter Johnson. [63]

On 8 February Keith Payne and his wife were woken by a deep humming sound. Looking out they saw a red glow that was so rich in colour it reflected on the water beneath. It was hovering above Angel Marshes in a straight line with, and right alongside, Blythburgh church of black dog fame.

On 24 February, postman Thomas Meyer was walking the deserted Sizewell beach with his dog, when a greenish/yellow 'pumpkin' flew in from the sea. It glowed 'like a television screen', sent his dog bolting in terror and left behind a pungent 'acid drops' odour, which suggests ozone created by the ionization effect of the glow. I gather that Mr Meyer suffered ill effects after the sighting and may not have been able to return to work.

The way in which these big cat/black dog sightings all inter-relate with UFOs, electrical effects, glowing eyes and pungent smells and in such narrowly defined 'window areas' certainly suggests that more than coincidence may be at work.

However, whilst Britain has been undergoing a veritable invasion of phantom cat sightings in the past few years, it is not alone. The phenomenon has a global perspective.

Loren Coleman reported on the number of 'maned' cat sightings in the USA. Witnesses generally believe these are mountain lions and they have been seen from east to west across the land. One sighting at Surprise, Nebraska, was especially apt![64]

Of course, some native big cats (but not lions) do exist in remoter parts of the USA; although these are all very much out of place. Coleman speculates that they are surviving 'fossil' relics.

However, far more commonplace (as in Britain) are the big, black cats that are usually interpreted as panthers. These appear in some very strange locations.

Ron Schaffner followed up a number of reports in the Ohio and Michigan areas and they were usually in downtown locations, e.g. outside stores or restaurants!

A flap concentrated on the late November/early December 1984 period and brought with it the usual controversy. Many eyewitnesses saw the creature close up and described it well as having a tail nearly three feet long and weighing in at around 150 lbs. The small village of Manchester, Michigan was inun-dated and despite the usual police efforts to capture it, only a few ambiguous paw prints turned up.

Cincinnati Zoo was sceptical that there would be the diet

required to keep such animals alive in the wild. The police began to have doubts, even though the quality of the witnesses existed whilst the hard evidence did not. And Schaffner discovered from the Ohio State Department of Natural Resources that they receive *weekly* stories of panther sightings but never investigate further because they are 'impossible'.[65]

Michael Goss is also very interested in the phantom cat sightings that dominate the Australian cryptozoological scene. We should bear in mind that Australia has its fair share of perfectly real strange wildlife and some of this can get confused with the phantoms. The dingo (or wild dog) is but one example. This is now accepted as the killer of a baby in the infamous recent case where the mother (played in the 'true story' movie by Meryl Streep) was at first charged with its murder. There were those who found it hard to believe in such things in modern times.

Australia is a country which loves practical jokes too. Michael Goss looked into the case of the monster of Minto that uttered bloodcurdling screams in the night and terrified residents. That was tracked down to a young lad who serenaded his girlfriend through a megaphone![66]

But our old friend the black panther is seen with regularity in the Southern Highlands of New South Wales, according to Paul Cropper, who has been out there on 'safari' looking for the non-existent creature.

He found one early case from 1966 (interestingly the stories begin in a similar period to the British examples from Surrey). Here a farmer near Nowra claims that his two dogs attacked a panther that came into the paddock. For their pains they were severely mauled.

Again there are occasional paw prints, one set of casts of these, but no other real evidence — except one rather interesting clue.

On 15 November 1977 Ramon and Tom Sega were hunting in the Cambewarra mountains when they saw the usual black panther with huge round eyes. Only this time they shot it — stone dead! Not realizing the importance of the event they simply skinned the beast and left the rest to rot. Cropper saw it two years later but said that it looked just like a large specimen of the feral (wild domestic) cat.

This revelation might be important. Are we to assume that

some people do not realize that wild domestic cats can look large and fierce and, fuelled by the rumours of panthers on the prowl, turn one into the other? In some cases that seems undeniable.

However, the real breakthrough (as it was touted) was to come with the Scottish big cat — Scotland being the one place, if you remember, where the true 'wild cat' (unrelated to wild domestics but much smaller than all the panther reports) still manages to survive.

The mystery cats have been seen in Scotland on a regular basis. Since a great deal of the land is rugged and unpopulated that is less unreasonable than in certain other venues. A good mini wave occurred in November 1979.

A train driver in Ross saw one on 3 November. There were many reports around Bettyhill — remember the UFO abductee? Up north, company director, Angus Monroe, nearly drove over a creature 'about the size of a Labrador dog, dark in colour but with a distinctive cat's face'. He added that the animal regularly appears during each early November — a new twist to the legend.

And so it went on. There were so many sightings in the first two weeks of November 1979 that the Aberdeen *Express* reported on 14 November how the Forestry Commission instructed rangers not to go out alone and to carry guns at all times.

A wave of sightings . . . forestry workers warned to be on guard . . . concentrating in an area named exactly the same as the first American witness to see a UFO, lose a period of time and become hailed an abductee . . . all focusing on the first two weeks of November 1979 in Scotland.

If these things have a paraphysical dimension and stay true to form the next move ought to have been predictable. But nobody seems to have spotted the connection.

At 10 a.m. on 9 November 1979, forestry worker Bob Taylor entered a clearing near Livingston with his dog beside him. Ahead appeared a strange object hovering low or on the ground. It seemed to fade in and out and be not quite real, but looked like a UFO. As he stood mesmerized two black 'things' a few feet in size emerged from its side and 'attacked' him. The last thing he recalled before losing awareness was a strange odour.

When he recovered some minutes later it was his dog that had brought him round. Bob was convinced that the animal had fightened the thing away. He was in a terrible state, weak and sick, and after dragging himself into his forestry vehicle found coordination so poor that he drove it into a ditch and had to stagger home.

The police were called and cordoned off the clearing. Marks on the ground were found. Bob himself went to hospital. His trousers were torn and he had scratch marks on his thighs. But he recovered very quickly. Later he underwent regression hypnosis to try to see if any new facts might be retrieved for the period when he either 'lost time' or was unconsious. The results of that session have never been made public and Bob seems unaware of the details himself.

This case made world headlines, was hailed as Scotland's first UFO abduction and was extensively (and very effectively) investigated by Steuart Campbell for BUFORA. He ultimately believed that Bob Taylor suffered hallucinations precipitated by a sort of epileptic attack, although Bob has no prior or subsequent history of this. Other UFO experts are convinced this was an aborted alien kidnap attempt, possibly thwarted by the dog. However, it actually does not fit the pattern for such reports too closely.[67]

To me the most fascinating aspect is the way it rounded off the conglomeration of Scottish big cat sightings almost to perfection. It was as if someone or something, somewhere or other was having a great big laugh at the expense of Scots people!

Such strange and crazy sidelines to the Scottish big cat were considered by few. Certainly not by BBC Television when its *Tomorrow's World* science magazine decided to make a documentary entitled *On The Trail of the Big Cat* which they screened on 22 May 1986.

The programme briefly surveyed the Surrey and Exmoor 'puma' reports and speculated about escaped zoo animals. Then it moved on to Scotland and deftly implied that the reports here were of the same sort of thing. In fact there are grounds for suspecting otherwise. Several dead cats from the Bettyhill region (known as the Kellas cat) had already been secured and, whilst black and fierce, were not large and looked similar to a wild domestic. However, it did suggest that the cat from this northerly location *was* completely physical and, with luck, could presumably be captured alive.

That is precisely what the BBC set out to do . . . and they succeeded.

Laying a special trap they captured what they described as a 'young, female Kellas cat'. However, zoological experts were quick to point out that it was not much bigger than a large domestic, and had several significant differences from the various dead Kellas cats.

Tomorrow's World conducted extensive tests on the living specimen housed at the Highland Wildlife Park. Chromosome analysis revealed what the BBC stated was the 'solution' to the mystery. The creature was a hybrid, formed by a wild domestic mating with the Scottish wildcats. The species were close enough for this to be possible, resulting in an entire new variety of creature.

But had the BBC finally resolved the matter? Karl Shuker, whom we met in the last chapter hunting aquatic monsters, surveyed those who were most involved after they had time to think. Nobody seemed to believe that the hybrid caught by the BBC *was* the Kellas cat.[68]

The witnesses said it was much too small, even given that it was a female. Edward Orbell, who was looking after the cat at the Wildlife Park, said it was in no way the same creature as those seen and killed in the Kellas/Bettyhill area. The Nature Conservancy Council dismissed it in cavalier fashion as just 'a moggy gone wild' and Kevin Duffy from Edinburgh Zoo later made known that the dead specimens *and* the one caught alive by the BBC were not the same thing as was being reported as a phantom panther. He agreed the live example *was* a hybrid and that these must exist in the wild, but that something else was apparently out there too.

So where do we stand? The Adswood, Stockport, case demonstrates that sometimes escaped big cats can create real sightings. But this must be very rare. The Cambewarra, Australian, skinned cat shows that ordinary domestics that are living wild (the ferals) could seem to be larger than they are and provide fuel for the flaps. Is that what the dead specimens from Kellas are? As for the live one, this is definitely a hybrid between ferals and wild cats — but there are no wild cats anywhere in Britain except in northern Scotland. So at the very best it can only explain these tiny few cases located here. And only these if we reject the views of the zoologists and witnesses who remain adamant that the live and dead Kellas cats are far too small to be what they saw.

In addition we have the problem of the rogue nature of the phantom felines. The experience in northern Scotland, where several dead cats and one live one were caught fairly easily with concerted effort, only throws into much sharper relief the incredible elusiveness of the world's other big cats.

If they are entirely real, then how do they avoid capture? What happens to their bodies? How do they survive? Why is there so little evidence? And how do we account for the animals' seemingly magical attributes and the curious comparisons between the phantom cat stories and other aspects of the paranormal, such as UFOs?

Responsible thinkers on the subject, like Michael Goss, have been forced away from the simplistic view that they are all real animals. He points out the importance of 'urban legends', where once a story turns into a set of rumours bordering on the legendary, a kind of cultural predisposition to make the legend come true begins to take over.

Yet there is also something going on at a deeper level of the mind. Those Bettyhill/Betty Hill type coincidences are suspicious. Michael Goss notes that in a typical flap of sightings at Fobbing, Essex, where a 'mountain lion' was reported, the village happens to sport a Lion Hill with the White Lion inn on top![69]

Clearly the big cats, like other monsters, are just as mysterious in the world of our minds as they are in the woods and forests of our planet.

4.

Sky Monsters

Just because a message comes from Heaven doesn't mean it isn't stupid.

Dr Jacques Vallée, computer expert and phenomenologist

In 1969 a Colorado University report costing millions of dollars at today's prices was published on behalf of the US Government. Often known as the Condon report, after Dr Edward Condon, the atomic physicist who supervised its two-year operation, this rather dismal effort had one primary task. It set out to examine the question of whether alien beings were visiting the earth by flying saucer.

This was a very odd stance to take as a first principle. Surely the correct scientific question was: do UFOs exist, and if so what possible explanations might there be for them? However, in 1969 most people found such a distinction academic. Even today the popular view seems to be that if you do not accept visitations by spaceship, then you are saying there is no such thing as UFOs: the two terms are interchangeable.

Yet many researchers who have devoted a great deal of time to the subject (such as myself) are convinced beyond reasonable doubt that these phenomena exist (but only as *unidentified flying objects* — nothing more). Other than that they are frequently dismissive, or in my case highly doubtful, that any of these UFOs are alien spacecraft.

The Condon team never understood this paradox. Yet strangely they offered powerful evidence in its favour. Examining just a few dozen cases their 1,000-page study still found *one third* of these which could not be accounted for in terms of known science. Often their summaries concluded with phrases that were far more outspoken than those forming conclusions to case reports from BUFORA's team of field investigators.[70]

This illustrates some interesting facets of the way in which science and society deals with anomalies. However, of more immediate note is the staggering number of UFO reports that are being made, all steeped in this modern mythology dictating that what is seen *are* alien spaceships.

BUFORA has over 10,000 cases on record for Britain alone. The Ministry of Defence retain sightings reported to them at least back to 1962. In recent House of Commons statements they have referred to sightings still coming in at the rate of about 400 per year, even during the eighties.

In a country such as the USA, where population and area are several times that of Britain, the figures are higher still — and it is easy to estimate the total number happening worldwide, especially when we appreciate that the UFO phenomenon is truly global. No country on earth has failed to generate sightings, from the remote Indonesian islands to the African bush and the frozen wastes of Antarctica. Wherever there are people there seem to be UFOs.

However, despite these hundreds of thousands of sightings that have now accumulated, the Condon study uncovered another key fact that has since been confirmed by Gallup Poll surveys: between 15 and 20 per cent of the population think they have seen something strange in the skies, but almost nine out of ten *never* say a word to anyone, except perhaps their immediate family.

This is by far the most widespread epidemic of monstrous visions running amok within today's world, yet we form our conclusions about it from just a fraction of the evidence.

Most material that we use to make judgements is heavily influenced by its commercial value. The serious tabloids reject the subject as 'occult nonsense' and the mass market ones are highly selective and tend to publicize only the sensational cases with the most unusual or ridiculous storylines. In such a fashion legends and stereotypes are born and prosper.

Research writers and UFO groups do their best through sober

ventures like the informative UFO Call, set up in cooperation with British Telecom and aiming 'to bring you the truth behind the headlines'. But the problem is that 5,000,000 people read 'I had sex with an alien' in a downmarket newspaper or buy the equivalent dubious book with its blanket marketing. A serious tome may reach 20,000 readers and create almost no publicity, because it is too 'dull' for the tabloids and too 'unscientific' for the highbrow press. It is rather like trying to dent a steamroller with a feather.

Naturally, the same sort of dilemma occurs with all monster phenomena. But the UFO mystery is the twentieth-century space-age supremo and attracts far more attention than the rest put together. Because of this saturation coverage, public attitudes are moulded by hysterical responses and that has a fundamental effect on how the phenomenon is both perceived and reported. I would argue it may also be fundamental to how the phenomenon manifests.

The 1988 production of a mass-market paperback by an American journalist shows this process in operation. The book came from one of the best-respected British publishing houses (Penguin), hardly noted for churning out literary trash. In this way, Gary Kinder's report on a Swiss 'yokel' who claimed to have seen and photographed UFOs achieved a respectability many other titles could never hope to emulate. I saw it in stores marketed as 'science' — which is stretching things! The cover also proclaimed it to be 'the best documented UFO case ever' which, to be charitable, might be termed artistic licence.

Here is a summary of that 'documented science'. A one-armed Swiss country man sets up a small philosophical group and travels around the world. Many of his neighbours seem to consider him eccentric, but he presents dozens of photographs in full colour of what look like the archetypal flying saucer of every conceivable variety. He sees these 'craft' often, but the villagers never seem to be there when they land. On this basis, people flock from all over the world, treating him as a guru.

'Billy' Meier, the witness, even named his son Atlantis, such is the grip of his new-found mythology. As the people come (including eventually mystic actress Shirley MacLaine, who allegedly weeded his garden) so his fame spreads and the stories become ever more fantastic. Now he travels in time to meet

Jesus. Trees are teleported into the past. He photographs 'God's Eye' and lets the aliens take him for a ride into the future where he can film San Francisco *after* the next earthquake. Unfortunately, someone later demonstrates that this 'photo' appears to be rather similar to a lifelike painting published in a magazine. Deftly, Billy explains that the aliens planted the correct vision of the future into the artist's mind and that is why the scenes are the same.

As to his photographs of 'beamships' from the 'pleiades' star cluster, he knows their origins because a beautiful, blonde-haired space alien talks to his mind. These photographs look pretty, but some cynics question why they seem to be taken looking straight at the sun or why people underneath a giant spaceship dangling precariously above their heads are ignoring this apparition and smiling into the camera lens instead.

On the back of the hardcover we find quotes from scientists, apparently endorsing the case. For instance, Dr Robert Post, head of NASA's photographic laboratory is quoted, seeming to suggest the images *do* show real UFOs. However, once we buy the book and scan through the assessments to find Dr Post's full statement (page 199), we discover that he was visually impressed with the photographs but they were not analysed. In fact, 'further scrutiny' could have seen them unmasked as fakes. Dr Robert Nathan, who developed the imaging technique at the lab, was even less impressed and decided not to devote time and money at the facility to study the pictures.[71]

I met Gary Kinder briefly in the USA soon after the book was published there. He struck me as being very sincere, but out of his depth in the complexities of this field. He had become entranced by the lure of this astonishing case, despite admitting that virtually every UFO expert he talked with advised him to stop wasting time on it. As a writer he had inevitably seen the commercial potential of a 'good story' but not yet learnt the hard way (as only time and experience allows) that there is a gulf — wider than the space between the pleiades — separating imaginative candyfloss like this and the hard stuff that constitutes the UFO phenomenon; and that to hype one seriously damages the other and badly affects innocent witnesses in the process.

Kinder's book carries several comments by the 'groupies' who promoted the Billy Meier case suggesting that UFO investigators were involved in a 'conspiracy of defamation' and their jealousy and bickering was what caused them to reject this 'evidence'. They neglect to point out that in their first reports, written years before the book came out, these objective investigators noted curious little items found within the case, such as the model UFOs discovered in Billy Meier's possession, or the computer enhancement analysis work of his photographs which indicated strongly that they may well be small objects crudely suspended in the air.

Jealousy and bickering does not come into it, but self-policing does. If a case has problems, this must be made clear by those who profess to be experts, otherwise, their judgement on more creditable stories will be called into question — and rightly so.

So if the kind of story that attracts the headlines and sells books is not what UFOs are all about — what is? Perhaps a letter to me from the USS *Enterprise*!

In case you are wondering, the author was not Captain Kirk. The USS *Enterprise* is an American ship, after which the *Star Trek* voyager was named. Ezra, otherwise a resident of New York City, wrote to me to report what he saw in the sky: 'I was watching TV in the living-room at night. I noticed a light, thinking it was a UFO. It turned out to be a helicopter. A lot of them were flying . . . Then I noticed a rocket-like thing all lit up with multicolour lights . . . The helicopters were all around it like they were escorting it.'

That is much more typical of the reports we receive by the truck load. We may speculate about military test planes, or weapons, and scan the data for a possible solution. Most of the time we find one; although the witness is not always persuaded by our sceptical detective work.

Back in Britain a journalist with the *Lancashire Evening Post* who was interviewing me for a story confided something that he had experienced. It was October 1977, about 6 p.m. during the evening rush hour. He was travelling home through Upholland near Wigan on the M6 motorway — one of the busiest in the land. Three white lights appeared in the sky, which lined up into a triangle as he watched them. They remained stationary in the air for well over a minute, then appeared to streak away very fast.

Given these circumstances there should be no doubts about

this case. Hundreds of other people surely saw the spectacle with him. Well, actually, no. So far as we can ascertain, *nobody* else did. One of the most curious features of these stories is the isolation factor. It is as if a personal display is put on for the witness in his or her own private movie theatre and nobody else is allowed to buy a ticket.

Ridiculous? Perhaps. But what are we to make of a further strange almost throwaway remark the journalist added? 'You know,' he told me, 'this is weird. I've never seen anything before, but during the couple of days leading up to this sighting I *knew* I was going to see something. Yet I totally forgot about it until afterwards. It was almost like I dreamt it and remembered only in my subconscious, until it then really happened.'

Switch continents and here is another case, reported by Christopher Markham* in Melbourne, Australia. His story is even less straightforward and with its telling our doubts and confusions can only grow.

Christopher believes that UFOs come from another dimension. He says this is the only explanation he can find for how they 'appear and disappear at random'. His evaluation was stimulated by a personal experience on 27 December 1987, when he was camping with his wife at Lorne, Victoria, on the coast to the south-west of his home city.

At dawn on that morning he was in a 'state of subliminal consciousness' (i.e. half awake/asleep). Suddenly he 'felt' a powerful force and 'from that moment I "saw" this object which I cannot describe'. He explains that he cannot describe it because 'I did not physically "see" . . . my state of consciousness enabled me to be aware of this thing.'

It passed over his head and he 'felt my skin being pulled outward . . . it emitted immense energy. I wanted to get up and look at this thing, but I was unable to. I "know" it was not a dream.'

He adds that nobody else on the beach saw it because he asked them. Now he thinks that it was something connected with his state of mind that caused him to be aware of the Lorne UFO, whereas everybody else was simply not tuned into this doorway between dimensions.

Once again we see how this latest 'monster' phenomenon, like all the others we have met, has its rock solid façade compromised by a mysterious subjective spectre.

Rockets, lights and presences in the sky might well seem a very long way from dinosaurs and phantom cats, but I hope that you already recognize the interplay which weaves these differing strands together. And as we progress through our study even UFOs should begin to take on attributes which may help quell your suspicions of irrelevance.

Firstly, let us get it clear that most UFO sightings reduce to IFOs (*identified* flying objects).

For instance I received a letter from a highly-qualified Ministry of Defence engineer, working on a site in Aldershot, Hampshire. On 8 June 1982 he had been on the Isle of Man and, like thousands of motorcycle enthusiasts packing the island for the annual TT, was at a vintage display in Mooragh Park, Ramsey. As it happens I was on the island myself that day, suffering the races to placate my other half. I can attest to the beautiful sunny weather and that nobody else apparently reported the UFO witnessed by this engineer.

However, in this case not *reporting* and not *seeing* the UFO were two quite different things.

What the witness described was this: a perfect white ring, not unlike one of the circles on the Olympic Flag, hanging in the trees above the park. He says that it drifted very slowly to the west and after a couple of minutes went out of sight, but not before he took two photographs with a good-quality camera plus 150mm zoom lens.

We have to look very closely at the pictures to find the ring, but it is there. Professional analysis of the film pronounced it genuine. Estimates suggest the UFO was about 30 feet in diameter.

Being on this small island when the events took place gave me an advantage I would not have had otherwise. I happened to have seen something around this time which I thought important. This was a Pitt Special aircraft doing flying displays. Whilst the photograph clearly is not of the aircraft, I recalled that it emitted smoke as part of its 'loop the loop' manoeuvres.

It was a simple matter to discover that the aircraft had flown over the park ten minutes before the photographs were taken. The air conditions were unusually hot and stable, and everything matched a ring being formed from the fuel vapour, trapped in a thermal between the hot air and the heat generated by hundreds of motorcycles and thousands of people. This fuel vapour, drifting just like a smoke ring blown out of a cigar, could easily create a puzzle for anyone who had not seen the aircraft emitting the residue.[72]

Fully 90 to 95 per cent of all UFO sightings can be explained either as simple mistakes or as sometimes quite bizarre examples. We have had owls eating fungi and glowing in the dark and a trained shaggy dog that masqueraded as an alien by walking on its hind legs through a Yorkshire town!

Sociologist Dr Ron Westrum points out that witnesses usually follow the 'escalation of hypotheses' in their efforts to find a solution, junking that answer when the UFO does not match up, and replacing it by something else until only an exotic solution will satisfy. Rarely is a UFO the first accepted notion. The trend is much more akin to someone saying, 'it's a bird, it's a plane — no, it's Superman!', as in comic-book lore.

However, when a witness does not incorporate what Dr Westrum calls 'reality checks' misperceptions are far more likely to occur.[73]

For instance, I saw a UFO in April 1978. I then lived at Irlam in Lancashire, on the edge of Chat Moss. Immediately I saw the orange light low over the horizon I began to adopt 'reality checks', measuring what I was seeing against aircraft, stars or other possibilities, then calling another witness to check what I was seeing. When it disappeared I stayed watching the twilight sky for some moments and so observed the sequel I would have missed had I left the scene immediately upon the 'UFO' doing a vanishing act.

A few yards from me a housewife was on the Moss with her dog and had seen it too. She was terrified and fled indoors with it still visible. I was unaware of her presence until a reporter visited me from the *Warrington Guardian* three days later. The housewife had reported not an orange light, but a saucer-shaped blob, which memory, expectation and journalistic prose quickly turned into a spaceship. Whilst I had discovered what the UFO was, partly through my observations and partly through subsequent enquiries, events had escalated, making the story into something far stranger than it was.

What was it then? After the orange blob vanished there was

a ten second gap and then blinking red, white and green lights appeared, slowly drifting off to the south — towards Manchester Airport, in fact. The UFO had been a helicopter that was crop spraying at a farm some distance away (far enough for no sound to be heard). The orange blob was the powerful searchlight it carried because there were electricity powerlines in the area and it was hovering low in semi-dark conditions. With the job done, the helicopter pilot switched this off, put its proper navigation lights back on and returned to base.

My awareness of the subject had ensured I carried out 'reality checks' and also helped me find the cause. This woman had jumped to the conclusion of a UFO and the media and the public wanted that too. After all 'woman sees spaceship' is news; 'woman misperceives helicopter' is not.

Of course, UFO sightings of mystery blobs in the sky are one thing. They are ten a penny and they represent by far the majority of reports. However, where the subject begins to overlap with the other types of monster we have looked at is when witnesses profess to observe not merely a funny light but an animate creature. In the parlance of the greatest of the pioneer UFO experts, the late Dr J. Allen Hynek (borrowed with millionaire-making opportunism by movie mogul Steven Spielberg) these are the 'close encounters of the third kind'.

For instance, there was the sasquatch riding a UFO near Sheffield, South Yorkshire.

Two courting teenagers, Robert Holmes and Sally Jensen, were parked in Myers Lane, Worrall, in a semi-rural area where plenty of odd things have happened down through the years. The romantic surroundings of the narrow lane contain a golf course and the council tip. But it does afford some sanctuary from prying eyes and is a favourite haunt of many of the locals.

We cannot be certain of the date. The estimate was April 1977, but as the sun had set and the witnesses refer to 'about 5 p.m.', this is simply not possible: either it was at least a couple of hours later or the date was two months earlier.

Sally heard a 'crackle', like somebody walking on leaves. She alerted Robert (who did not hear this noise). Both then saw what they took to be 'continental headlights' approaching them from behind. As the lane was narrow they were concerned about there being sufficient room for the vehicle to pass. But they soon realized it was no vehicle. Ambling down the path towards them was a hemispherical dome, bright orange in colour, and with a gigantic black figure stood face on as if pressed against the outer skin of a 'half moon'. Later, after watching an episode of *The Six Million Dollar Man*, which had 'bigfoot' mixed up in the plot, they remarked that the entity was very similar in appearance.

The 'man' was about ten feet tall, looked 'frizzy' and 'rough' and was surrounded by a white 'aura'. He seemed to be walking in their direction at the same time as the whole thing made steadily towards their car.

Whilst the dome overlapped the edge of the road, such was its size, no illumination was cast down. On a 'strange impulse' (*very* strange given the circumstances) Robert switched on the car radio. Sally noted: 'It was terrible. We knew the radio had worked before we got there.' Now it was full of a persistent crackle. It was switched off immediately.

Convinced the best plan was to escape, Robert crashed the car through the gears and took off at 70 m.p.h. down the lane. They quickly passed another car that was just off the road ahead of them. Yet despite their speed, the dome and figure seemed to retain the same distance behind them. By the end of the lane car headlights were visible between their position and the UFO. They took this to mean the other car had seen it and was on the move.

Robert shot round the bend, then cursing himself, reversed quickly. Within a minute or so he was back at the lane end. The other car had certainly not emerged and there was no other turn off, unless it had reversed around and headed straight at 'bigfoot' and his personal UFO. However, neither car nor apparition were visible.

Robert drove a very nervous Sally home. They did report it to the local paper, but someone there explained: 'If we publish this we will get all sorts of people reporting all sorts of things to us.'

There is no doubt that this encounter frightened these young people. Nigel Watson, who interviewed them and investigated, commented that he found them 'pleasant, honest and friendly'. But what on earth did they see?

They followed the 'reality check' pattern, e.g. by speculating that metal on the council dump had created the radio interference. And their first reaction (a car or truck headlight) is further evidence of that. Yet the way in which the object resembled the setting sun, swollen near the horizon, and the 'following us without getting closer' observation, both fit in with something far distant in the sky. This leaves us very confused. Just how could they make such a bizarre mistake?

It has happened. In one case remarkably similar to this, a woman at Bignall End in Staffordshire saw an orange dome with a silhouetted alien in front. An astronomer at Keele later demonstrated with reasonable certainty that she must have seen the moon near the horizon with a telegraph pole in front of it creating the illusion of an alien!

Interestingly, on 14 April 1977, at sunset, a florist and her husband in Chester reported a big orange dome on the horizon and for some reason they seem to have mistaken the sun. Possibly unusual atmospheric conditions were involved. But if so, why didn't thousands of people see the effect?

Robert Holmes made an interesting comment to the investigator about this Worrall encounter. Thoroughly bemused, as are we all, he noted a gut feeling that the thing was not three-dimensional or solid but 'it could have been a projection from something', like a laser beam or searchlight directed onto cloud, but with very mysterious purposes.

A hoax by a third party? A reaction test by psychologists? Who can say. But it shows once again that we can never take anything at face value. And, of course, the 'projection' might have come from somewhere nearer at hand — the minds of the witnesses themselves.[74]

We can find plenty of entity sightings that are on the borderline between UFO encounters and other monsters. They are reported as UFOs purely because of the latters' popularity in modern times.

The dreadful experience of Cheshire service engineer, Ken Edwards, at Risley in March 1978 is a case in point. The glowing white figure he saw had attributes of a ghost, passing straight through a security fence into an atomic energy research centre. Yet it had UFO close encounter features too (e.g. 'exploding' his van transceiver radio with a huge power surge and creating an apparent time lapse which was never unravelled). The media clearly hung it on the peg of ufology by instantly reporting it as a 'spaceman', even though no UFO was seen and they were completely unaware of the high incidence of UFO sightings that surrounded the apparition. Tragically, the witness contracted multiple cancers soon after and died a young and baffled man. We never resolved this case. [75]

Over in New Zealand, in January 1969, a man and wife at Whangamata had an experience, recounted in a catalogue of such cases compiled by skilful Australian researcher Keith Basterfield. They were on a beach when there was 'an uncanny silence' and 'a feeling of wrongness in the air' (familiar to us from other cases as the remarkably consistent Oz factor). Suddenly a group of tall figures 'floated down some nearby sandhills'. Their extremities were not visible. And the only clue linking it with UFOs was a small 'balloon' that appeared for an instant between the figures and the witnesses, just before they not surprisingly turned and fled. [76]

These are representative of many other stories. There is no doubt that plenty of cases are being interpreted as UFO-related and therefore reported to UFO channels when in other circumstances they would have an entirely different kind of monstrous evaluation.

The Oz factor clue, which seems common to many monster stories, may well indicate that the witness enters an altered state of consciousness. However, the often associated 'time lapse' (where, more correctly, *sense* of time is affected) takes on dramatic importance in the UFO field. Witnesses can easily be convinced they have had part of their life stolen from their memory.

Here is a case that highlights the situation. It came to me from Jackie, a young woman who is English and lives in the Midlands. She comes from an excellent background (her father is a retired doctor) and has professional qualifications. During her childhood in Amherst, Nova Scotia, she had repeated dreams of UFOs which were full of strange feeling and a sense of 'I know these craft', although she had not consciously seen any UFOs.

Then, in 1979, near somewhere called 'Jerry's Ball Park', she was with a friend when a golden star appeared in the sky. They watched in astonishment as it fell down towards them (the expression 'like a lift out of control' was graphically used by one witness to describe this common phenomenon). It now resolved as an absolutely huge triangle that drifted very slowly away. Clear hints of Oz factor are once again present in her story, indicating that neither witness was experiencing normal consciousness during this experience. And Jackie notes that: 'there seems to be a memory gap . . . We saw the light drop and move towards us, and we saw it overhead flying away . . . But I do not recall the pieces in between.'

Also, Jackie has always found it odd that a kind of 'block' affected both of them afterwards. It was as if there was a pact not to talk or even think about the experience until years later. Indeed, her friend (who still lives in Canada) seems to retain this 'block' (which I have seen in plenty of other cases). Although she and Jackie correspond often the Canadian woman completely avoids any reference to the UFO.[77]

The standard remedy for a case like this is to take the witness to a psychiatrist (or, even more dangerously, an investigator performs the 'cure' his or herself without medical qualification). Here a hypnotic trance is induced to 'regress' the individual back to the experience and see if he or she can recall what happened during the 'gap'. In a large percentage of cases something is recalled, and that something is a supposed kidnap by the UFO entities, with a medical examination or other things performed 'on board' their craft.

A highly persuasive similarity exists between these cases, although the differences are as marked and as important. There are particular differences between countries (e.g. British 'aliens' are often taller, more human-like and not infrequently female, whereas American ones tend to be small, grey-skinned, almost always male and pretty clinical).[78]

The hypnosis craze was introduced first in the mid-sixties on the Betty Hill case (which you may recall through its name link with the Scottish phantom cats). Then the Condon report initiated regular work through regression of a police officer who lost only a few minutes during a sighting. However, it was New York artist Budd Hopkins who established himself as the doyen of this field, and his best-selling books about the cases he has studied have now made known to all Americans the accepted results of such experiments. They have even featured in the soap opera *Dynasty* so nobody can be immune![79]

Because of this, very little thought is given to the question 'should we hypnotize?' It is regarded as the obvious road to the truth, even though it often takes an outsider to appreciate that the 'missing time' can just as easily be manufactured in an artificial way out of the subconscious enthusiasm surrounding the case. This seems to imply that no alien entity story can be up to much *unless* it involves time 'stolen' by the space people and 'memories' (or fantasies?) stimulated through an induced state of consciousness — a state, bear in mind, where the wit-

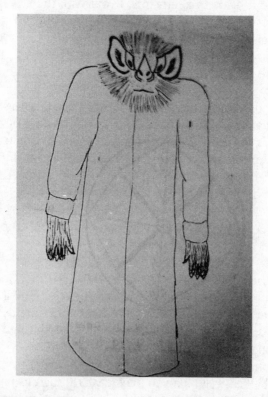

In October 1974 in Aveley, Essex, a British family claimed to have encountered a blue light, then a glowing greenish mist on a country road. Electrical interference affected their car and on arrival home over an hour and a half had vanished. Subsequent nightmares, researched under careful supervision by Andy Collins and others, revealed memories of an abduction by strange creatures such as this. These monsters allegedly performed medical examinations on the two adults present. In the years since then many other cases have come to light from all over the world (*Andy Collins, UFOIN/BUFORA*).

ness is under tremendous psychological pressure to 'come up with the goods' and so 'recall' an abduction.

In Britain, whilst quite a few of these 'hypnotic regression experiments' have been carried out (and I have attended several and served as a guinea pig in one), it remains the exception rather than the rule. I believe it is going to be useful to compare 'pre-hypnosis' cases (such as the Risley 'ghost' and the Amherst, Nova Scotia story) with the data base being developed from hypnosis sessions and their almost universal remembrance (or manufacture) of so-called 'hidden' memories.

This can then all be crossreferenced with Australia, where hypnosis is not used as a matter of principle. Researchers here believe that this would only further confuse what are already confusing stories. For this they do have justification, although I feel the existence of the two extremes (from Australia and the USA) and the halfway house approach of Britain provides an ideal basis for somebody to figure out just what is going on.

Unfortunately, whilst the USA is besotted with 'little grey men from outer space' and Australia (and to much the same degree Britain) has complete conviction that it's *all* in the mind and 'merely' hallucinations, I do not think we will get to the truth. Neither raw solution seems to work.

Having said that, it is obvious that the 'alien abduction' is going to be the subject placed to the fore of investigation in the nineties. Several major Hollywood movies on the theme were in preparation during 1989 and books on the subject have been achieving best-seller status, even though they pander to the attitude 'let's give the public what they want to hear'.

At present we see that the UFO phenomenon consists of a large mass of misperceptions and stray blobs. The 'alien contact' stories are only a small fraction of these, but as more and more exotic stories are explored, as more and more time lapses are discovered and subjected to hypnosis, the abduction is (wisely or not) being given precedence over everything else. We are now in danger of grossly overstating its significance.

It is very useful to look at what was probably the last abduction fully explored before the spring of 1987. That date is significant because it brought best-selling books, the *Dynasty* episodes and Budd Hopkins' appearance on almost every TV chat show under the sun. Abductions in the wake of this can only be treated as contaminated. But will they differ markedly from those which came before?

The most open-minded first-hand investigator of abductions in the USA is D. Scott Rogo, from John F. Kennedy University in California. His many years of experience in psychology and parapsychology enable him to see that the simple alien kidnap theory is just too pat and does not fit the facts. Indeed, he knows (just as I have found from my experience in the field) that the truth about these abductions must be *far* stranger than that.

The witness to this story is an Hispanic man named Sammy Desmond.* He comes from Los Angeles, but his encounter took place at his nearby family home in Reseda, in the San Fernando Valley.

Sammy has a history of strange experiences. These began with bedroom apparitions of a floating 'being made out of fog' and, later, childhood experiences of a poltergeist nature, where metal objects used to bend and break in his proximity. Eventually he became regularly plagued by small lights, several inches in diameter, which would invade his room at night and leave him paralyzed. His only escape was to leap up screaming, a fact that other members of his family well remember.

Most American abduction researchers totally reject this idea of a 'psychic track record' that seems to follow a witness throughout his or her life. But I found it repeated in British cases and have no doubt whatsoever of its vital relevance to our understanding of the problem.

Indeed, one Welsh case about which I wrote an entire book has so many similarities with Sammy Desmond's story that it virtually confirms the pattern to be of great significance.[80]

In the winter of 1984, when Sammy was 30, his father was dying of cancer, possibly an important psychological trigger. The experiences with the bedroom lights heightened to a point where around 2 a.m. one night he entered a 'weird mood', as he terms his altered state of consciousness. He pre-empted their arrival, effectively invoked them upon himself and let the process continue. Instead of resisting when they descended onto his body he let the paralysis and dizziness take over. Suddenly he saw a light fly out of the closed window. It was morning. Six hours had apparently disappeared. However, when he took a shower he found marks on his navel and a strange fluid oozing out. Other family members saw this. Later he encountered more lights and 'small humanoids' out in the yard.

Sammy approached Scott Rogo with this story in January 1987 and wanted hypnosis to try to plug the gap. Dr Rogo arranged for the first session to be conducted by Dr Thelma Moss, a former university pyschologist. She was given no indication that a UFO abduction was suspected, and remember that no UFO was reported by Sammy. Indeed, he had placed a 'demonic' interpretation on the events.

Three other later hypnosis sessions were carried out by Scott Rogo himself and a fairly comprehensive account emerged. The transcript reproduces a scenario I have heard from the lips of half a dozen British abductees whilst undergoing hypnosis, even though Dr Rogo satisfied himself that Sammy had no (conscious) knowledge of other cases and certainly possessed no books on the subject.

Sammy felt a 'tingle' over his body, then a 'floating' and he just 'found himself' in a strange, softly-lit room without sharp angles. He was on a small table or bed in the middle of the room. The absolute terror that poured out from the initial contact was now more subdued, as if by magic.

Again, this entire plotline has been precisely reproduced in British abduction cases, such as that of Yorkshire police officer Alan Godfrey.

Sammy was surrounded by a group of figures of the classic American type (and this part is the only major deviation from British data). They are about four and a half feet tall, with bald egg-shaped heads, hardly any nose and a very 'flat' face. The most disturbing thing about abductions is the way in which so many of them feature almost direct reproductions of the same very limited entity types. Nobody gets kidnapped by alien giraffes or baby elephants (both alien monster-types invented by science-fiction authors in two of the biggest selling 'alien kidnap' novels of recent years).

Ultimately, Sammy had a long needle poked into his navel; he was shown 'films' on a TV screen beside him; much interest was displayed by the aliens in his reproductive organs; and he was eventually 'floated' back into the house. Those already aware of abductions will yawn at the familiarity.

Perhaps the most interesting point Scott Rogo notes is that

shortly after this information emerged under hypnosis, Mrs Desmond, Sammy's mother, was able to describe some of the detail. She apparently had no knowledge of the hypnotic results but said that in the few hours/days after the incident, when the physical marks were found on her son's body, he *told* her of the abduction experience. Evidently, he forgot this very quickly, in the same sort of way we forget our dreams. Even when Mrs Desmond reported what her son told her, Sammy still could not recall having conscious memory of the abduction at any time prior to the hypnosis.[81]

How do we determine whether there is a continuum between the seemingly unrelated blobs of light in the sky and highly complex and disturbing experiences such as Sammy Desmond's?

We saw clues that there might be from Jackie's encounter in Canada, where the same sort of temporary memory block occurred. We also found Sammy's strange behaviour reproduced in other cases (e.g. the Worrall 'sasquatch'). It is almost as if something is taking control of the conscious mind of the witness and making him or her do things which later seem out of place and bizarre under the circumstances.

But does this control come from outside the witnesses or from their own subconscious?

I think we can see the answer to this question by the way in which cases blend into one another.

There is no doubt that some kind of atmospheric energy phenomenon is involved in many reports. Whatever causes it, this is physically real.

At just after 9 a.m. on the morning of 11 January 1973, building surveyor Peter Day succeeded in taking a movie film of a yellow-orange ball of light moving low across tree tops on the Oxfordshire/Buckinghamshire borders. Forty minutes later a US Air Force jet crashed mysteriously in flames a few miles away. It has not been made public what happened, although the pilot ejected and used a new rocket-propelled parachute system to survive. This incident is undeniably real. There were even independent witnesses to the ball. I was at a private seminar in London which Kodak set up after analysing the film and pronouncing it genuine. A dozen leading scientists and atmospheric physicists from universities and academic research establishments such as Harwell were invited to study the evidence outside the glare of publicity. Most turned up. None had a satisfactory solution to offer. All refused the suggestion (with the approval of Peter Day) that they take the film back to their labs. 'You don't expect us to show *this* to our colleagues?' one enquired of me.[82]

A similar multi-coloured (greenish, orangey, fiery-red) 'blob' (as good a name as any and less presumptive than UFO) appeared from over Pendle Hill in Lancashire at just after 3 a.m. on the morning of 9 March 1977. Two factory workers saw it and felt an enormous pressure pushing them into the ground. There was also a tingling sensation and 'hair on end' effect that indicates the phenomenon was generating an electrostatic field. (You can sense this prickling if you put your arm next to a TV screen that has just been switched off.) The car engine and lights on the vehicle they drove underneath the blob both cut out and only returned to life later, when the thing drifted away making a quiet humming noise. The two men later felt ill, with pounding headaches and watering eyes. This case is by no means an isolated example. It is typical of several hundred 'vehicle interference' stories now on record from around the world.[83]

Six months later, on 17 September 1977, a young couple renovating an old post office in the tiny Cornish village of Newmill confronted another blob at very close proximity. The woman 'felt a sensation', turned and saw a greenish haze floating towards her. Her boyfriend rushed outside and he now saw the green oval drifting around the steps. Eventually it floated off over the wall, now tinged with red, meandered around some trees and finally disappeared after more than half an hour. Within a week both of the couple became ill. The vomiting, muscular pains and headaches were enough to put them both in hospital. Despite extensive tests the cause was never revealed, although it has many similarities to exposure to certain forms of radiation. The woman even had a healthy appendix removed, such was the bafflement of the doctors. You have no doubt recognized the similarity with the greeny-yellow object seen on the beach near the nuclear reactor in East Anglia, as reported in Chapter 3 in connection with 'black dogs'.[84]

From this small sample we can clearly see that the form of UFO otherwise known as a blob must be physically real, with associated radiation, and generating electrostatic and other effects on anyone or anything that gets too close. But scientists run away from this evidence because to them it is all tarred with the brush of crazy UFO tales.

These symptoms cover the majority of the puzzling effects we can find in close encounter cases, with the exception of the appearance of alien entities. But are such stories completely different, or somehow related to the blobs? Do the blobs 'turn into' aliens through a strange process of perception, imagination or reality attunement?

This is just a possibility to bear in mind, because otherwise we must have two separate phenomena: the completely real blobs, and the alien contacts of more doubtful objectivity. Yet the aliens share so many of the same physical attributes (stopping car engines and lights, creating tingles and hair-on-end effects and sometimes leaving induced 'radiation sickness') that if there is no relationship between the two this coincidence is very puzzling.

And yet the blobs are reported so consistently. For instance, here is an excellent example investigated by Eric Morris, again in Cornwall, at another small village known as Colan.

The witness was a nursing assistant and was travelling to work at 5.45 p.m. on 6 February 1985 when she saw a bright yellowish blob beside the road. It was 'oval, about ten feet long and seemed to be "bobbing" as it moved', developing a more fuzzy/hazy aura as it passed low along the hedgerows by the perimeter of an RAF base (!) and turning greenish with a red central section, then purple, and finally just vanishing. This remarkable colour sequence suggests to some researchers that it slowly altered its frequency of radiation through the spectrum to violet and then on to ultra-violet, at which point it became invisible. However, once invisible it may have been all the more dangerous, possibly radiating in more harmful frequencies. Another clue is that when the ball floated past a cottage with a white wall it unexpectedly cast an *orange* shadow onto it.

What is worth noting here is that those scientists tempted to dismiss blobs as 'just' ball lightning (a rare and still mysterious atmospheric plasma) should consider the witness in this last case. She has *seen* ball lightning. It came in through her kitchen as a tiny lump and exploded right in front of her mother and herself. She is adamant that the Colan blob bore no comparison in any sense.[85]

This remarkable consistency of account in case after case is what makes me sure of my conviction that the blob is very real. It is a type of what we call UAP (unidentified atmospheric phenomenon). But this very consistency makes it difficult to understand how the blob could possibly generate those more bizarre alien contact stories, in which it is certainly not being reported with even passing accuracy, if it be the source.

The answer to our dilemma can best be found in the intermediary cases: those where things other than blobs seem to be involved, but they are not quite archetypal alien contacts of the form — a spaceship landed, out popped a little alien and waved hello.

Sam wrote to me from a small town in Western Australia. He wanted to ask 'if I'm a little mad or if I'm just different from others'. Certainly his letter was unusual, explaining that he had just bought one of my brand new books but had first 'read' it (in a dream) two years earlier (i.e. *before* I had started to write it!).

It is Sam's dreams which most concern him. These are on the borders of reality. He does not know if they are real or a dream, even after he 'wakes up'. Often they involve UFOs. On at least one occasion they included 'waking' in the night to find a small dark shape, the size of a child, standing right next to his bed. Thinking it was his brother he called out, but the shape just dissolved into the night.

His most vivid UFO dream goes like this: 'I was lying in a white room on top of a white table. I remember the room was fairly cool and there was a smell like in hospitals, only not as strong. I remember I was completely naked and I felt extremely light-headed and floaty. There were figures or shadows (four I think) standing around the table, but they were standing away from it, so I couldn't really see them. I had a feeling of being touched but I don't recall where or by what. I don't really remember anything after that, but I do remember everything was so vivid it seemed real.'

Sam says he is not psychic (but then describes frequent out-of-body sensations, apparent telepathic experiences and having seen a number of apparitions!). He also has a strange inner belief that seems to exist in his subconscious but cannot be brought to the surface. This indicates that certain events are meant to unfold and *will* unfold according to a hidden plan. There are trigger objects involved, including 'a pair of earrings . . . long, blue with blue stars on the end . . . about seven of them'.

I have noticed this same compulsion with other witnesses. They feel sure that more information is locked inside them and will only be released once the time is right. Whatever this means (perhaps an allegory for the concept that the truth about these experiences lies *within* themselves and not in outer space?) then it is a pattern to be understood.

Of course, sometimes witnesses invoke their own beliefs in order to explain their experiences. How would you interpret the following story, for example?

A middle-aged woman sits in her garden at Blairgowrie, Scotland, on the warm, sunny afternoon of 25 April 1984. She is doing a religious tapestry of the Madonna. Her collie dog snoozes beside her. Suddenly, he leaps up, tail between his legs and scuttles indoors. As the lady looks up in surprise a ball of white light materializes out of thin air near her head and then 'enters' her. Temporarily blinded she feels calm and 'beautiful' until a white vaporous glow ascends from her and heads for the nearby bushes.

On the road to Damascus two thousands years ago such an event would have a clear explanation. However, the story is not so simple in the 1980s nor is it yet over. The cloud flashes like a lighthouse beacon and illuminates a UFO that is hovering over the fir trees at the end of the garden. The silvery object is shaped not unlike a (rather symbolic) key. The white cloud was moving over the shape illuminating it point by point.

The lady, who had now walked 'mesmerized' towards it called out to her son, who was around the front of the house; 'I bet you don't know what I'm looking at.' He came rushing around, but just as he arrived, the object and glow started to 'sway' then vanished in a pink flash. The son says he saw the flash (but nothing else) and found his mother staring transfixed at the trees.

We might regard this as an amusing anecdote, but the witnesses did not. They were sufficiently disturbed to call the police, who sent two officers to take statements and inspect the garden. The police reported it to RAF Leuchars, who called next day to say they could do nothing about it. Yet, less than a month later a strange unmarked helicopter circled the garden several times, very low. As it passed the trees where the UFO had been, both witnesses say it 'dipped'. The side doors were open and a red 'glow' came out. Two days later the helicopter returned for a single brief overpass. Attempts to discover whether the RAF or some other government body were checking with specialist equipment for possible effects left by the UFO received a curt refusal to cooperate.

It is tempting to think that someone, somewhere was sufficiently convinced by this experience to believe that physical evidence might have been left behind. Yet Steuart Campbell, who investigated the case, merely concluded it was possibly a form of hallucination. Indeed, perhaps it was, but that evades all the interesting questions brought to light.[86]

Of course, those who study the subject in a superficial way do so still under this spell of alien visitors. It seems such a logical answer, and it is what the phenomenon itself often claims. So, why is it difficult to believe that these alien monsters are not precisely that — visitors from beyond the earth?

There are a number of damning reasons we should briefly consider.

For a start, there are times when a seemingly good case owes its origin to something much less concrete. For instance, take some press reports which appeared in February 1988 about a woman in Lancashire who had supposedly been kidnapped by 'extra-terrestrial toyboys'!

Of course, we immediately recognize the tabloid sensationalism, but the story behind the nonsense at first sounds impressive. The woman had awoken in the night, floated out into the open, been led up a ramp into a UFO and given a medical examination inside a big white room by figures who smelt of cinnamon and had leathery skins.

Superficially there is little to distinguish this from many other cases and in that way it sounds persuasive. But there are crucial clues left out by this highly selective version of the facts.

I was first alerted the very same morning the incident happened by the man to whom the abductee had rushed straight round (a close friend and neighbour of hers, and a UFO investigator). I had arranged for a couple of reliable BUFORA investigators to be on scene within days and they had quickly concluded precisely what I did as soon as I heard of the incident.

Between 8 and 9 p.m. on the night of the abduction the woman had watched a TV programme. This was an episode of the soap opera *Dynasty* which featured Fallon Colby recalling her abduction aboard a UFO. She was led up a ramp. Her captors had leathery skin and smelt of cinnamon. The various links were so close that only one conclusion was possible. Whilst the woman may well have had a sincere experience of a vivid nature it must be based in some way on the TV show that she had watched hours before.

This conclusion is enforced because later under hypnosis far more details emerged. Several of them were points only found in the TV episode and rarely, if ever, in real cases. The alien even gave its name to her as 'Gerard' — one of the characters in *Dynasty*!

Another worrying factor about these cases is the veritable menagerie of alien monsters that tend to be involved. If we were being visited by space probes it is highly unlikely that more than one, or at most two, separate races would be coming here. Yet, apart from cases where a stereotyped figure seems to be reinforced (such as above) there are simply dozens of different kinds of aliens in the records and new ones are always turning up.

Here are just a very few examples. In Felling, Tyne and Wear, England, June 1964, several little humanoid creatures were seen cavorting about on a haystack. They had hands which glowed like light bulbs and were only two feet tall.

In Paciencia, Brazil, September 1977, several weird robotic figures four feet tall appeared. They had pointed heads, scaly skin, and stood on one 'pedestal' around which they could rock like a wobbly toy.

Over in Marzano, Italy, in December 1978 a security guard confronted a huge figure more than eight feet tall with three eyes, horned ears and triangular features. It looked like the creature from the black lagoon.

Meanwhile, on Ilkley Moor, West Yorkshire, England in December 1987 a former policeman saw (and photographed!)

a four-foot-tall figure that looked a bit like ET — dark green, with huge, pointed ears, long loping arms and claw-like feet.

All these cases were directly connected with UFOs (i.e. a UFO was seen by the witnesses and assumed to be the origin of the creature). It takes an extremely devoted believer in the extra-terrestrial theory to see in such an astonishing range of alien lifeforms true visitors who are coming here on intergalactic package tours.

It should also be noted that, whilst they vary, they do so still within the fairly basic confines of a humanoid shape. So, on the one hand they are too varied and on the other they are not wildly imaginative enough.

Compare and contrast this with reports of other monster types. Here too we find standardization but plenty of variation on a well-worked theme.

I mentioned a photograph of an alien. Surely that alone is sufficient to prove their reality? Well, as we might suspect from photographs of other monsters, it does not come close to doing so.

I am aware of about half a dozen pictures which supposedly show aliens. They vary as widely as the eyewitness reports. Some are now exposed as crude hoaxes (e.g. one boy photo-graphed a toy soldier and another a doll!) Hardly any stand up to much scrutiny.

Whilst the Ilkley Moor case has been extensively investigated by Peter Hough and the analyses of the photograph by experts (including the Kodak labs in Hemel Hempstead) do demon-strate that it does show a figure on the hillside, these assess-ments cannot distinguish between a real green ET and someone (such as a child) dressed up in a suit. Unfortunately, the photo-graph is too dim and fuzzy to tell us much more than that and the story, as always, has both its strengths and its weaknesses.

Certainly from my involvement (I have met the witness and helped Peter on some of the work) I could not put my reputation on the line by supporting its veracity. It could be that someone hoaxed the witness, or all of us, for reasons we might hypothe-size (e.g. to test our responses or investigational competence).

The same is true of every one of the tiny number of alien photographs. We have thousands of photographs of UFOs. We have dozens of pictures of one single lake monster (Nessie). Yet

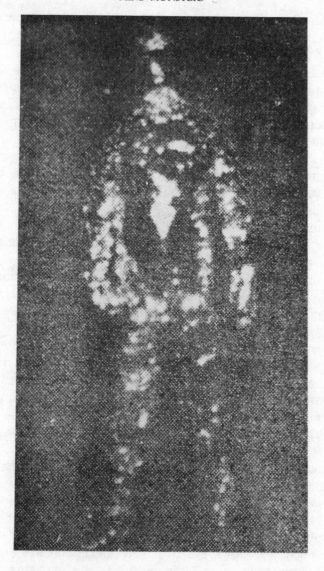

Police Chief Jeff Greenhaw from Falkville, Alabama, was called out by an anonymous report of a UFO. This was during a major wave of sightings in the USA throughout mid October 1973. He saw no UFO but did encounter this figure in a silvery suit, of which he took several photographs. Whilst there are some who suggest that the policeman was 'hoaxed' (i.e. the figure could be someone dressed up in a fireman's suit) it remains one of the few interesting photographs of a 'sky monster' (*Jeff Greenhaw*).

world wide over half a century we have accrued less alien photographs than we can count on the fingers of both hands. Nobody has yet answered *why* to my satisfaction.

So, if not photographic proof of aliens, is there any other kind of proof? We have had very few cases where anybody was given something by the aliens. An American man received two pancakes once (he ate one — it tasted like cardboard). When analysed, there was nothing unearthly about the other.

Philip Taylor, a college lecturer who coordinates investigations for BUFORA, studied another strange case of this type. The witness is a retired audiologist who, after rising to the rank of major in the army, specialized in research into hearing loss. He lived in a remote cottage near Hastings in Sussex and in 1967 had a series of encounters he only reported years later.

Edwin, the witness, claims nine visits by aliens between 17 August and 23 September. They were of small to normal height, very thin but with greyish 'parchment' skin and without hair, eyebrows or lashes. Their hands were like 'withered leaves' to the touch. They left in an arrowhead-shaped device, from the base of which emerged a blue glow. They communicated only by whistles and hisses.

On one occasion they stayed for hours, watched TV with him, took some fruit and tried a sip of whiskey (which they hated). They removed plant samples from the garden, then asked to take his dog away! He refused, and so they took some china model dogs instead.

In return for these gifts Edwin received some seeds and some crystals from the aliens. He planted the seeds and said a strange 'cactus-like' plant grew. This died long before he ever reported the experience and he did not photograph it. However, the crystals are a different matter. They looked a bit like uncut diamonds and so — possibly in hope — he sent one to a London diamond merchant who told him it was just quartz.

Edwin still had the crystal in 1986 and let Philip Taylor send it for analysis to the Institute of Geological Studies in London, from where as R.K. Harrison confirmed: 'Your specimen is a piece of glassy quartz — certainly not extraterrestrial, I am sorry to say.'

Edwin says he cannot understand why the aliens gave him such useless evidence, but sticks firmly to his story. Philip checked every angle he could and found a number of things that verified the witness as being truthful. But as the investigator was ultimately forced to conclude: 'I have not been able to disprove anything, neither have I been able to prove that anything unusual happened. This series of entity encounters must remain as simply a sincerely-believed experience.'

Unfortunately, the same statement might be made about any number of cases like it. Nothing demonstrably alien has ever been connected with a case. And although a number of witnesses allege physical effects after an encounter, as we have already seen, this means nothing more than a real cause for the effect — certainly not an extraterrestrial cause.

I could go on citing clues such as these for many pages. There are several others that stand out from the data. Why do multiple-witness cases so rarely share absolutely identical experiences during the missing time? Why has no third party ever witnessed somebody else being abducted? Why do these messages uttered by the aliens follow our earthly preconceptions and often include completely nonsensical science (e.g. in one story, light years were talked of as a time duration when a space traveller would surely realize they are a distance!)

I think the answer to all of these questions is inescapable. It is because in some way or another the experience depends upon the person who is experiencing it. At least part of it comes from within, rather than without, although I think it is very unwise to conclude that this is the more important part, or that these cases have no physical reality.

Dr Jacques Vallée, a computer scientist who has written several perceptive books on the subject, is convinced the UFO phenomenon is not what it seems. He said in a recent London lecture: 'If UFOs turn out to be simply extraterrestrial I will be very disappointed. I think I can come up with a much better answer than that.'

Vallée's answer can be summed up by the words of the French scientist Lacombe in the movie *Close Encounters of the Third Kind*. Lacombe (played by François Truffant) was meant to *be* Vallée, as a kind of UFOlogist's 'in-joke'. At one point in the script he explains that the compulsion felt by the witnesses to follow an image in their heads (of the Devil's Tower, Wyoming) is at the very essence of the mystery. 'It is a sociological phenomenon' he cries.

Indeed, in his work Vallée suggests an extradimensional reality might lie behind the reports: something we cannot perceive directly, but which is influencing social behaviour and cultural changes like a thermostat regulates the temperature in a central-heating system.

I believe Vallée is one of the few scientists who understands the significance of these cases and fully appreciates that there are no straightforward solutions. When the answer comes (if indeed it ever does come, as retaining the mystery might be part of its function) then it will likely be of fundamental importance to mankind; far more important than the revelation that we have visitors from alpha centauri.

There clearly has to be some link between these cases and the consciousness of the percipient. Too often they are symbolic. Too frequently we find curios and coincidences. It is possible to analyse these UFO stories like some psychologists analyse our dreams. Yet it is all too easy to let that recognition provide an easy escape route via cries of 'it's all in the mind'. The facts plainly argue otherwise. The physical dimension of the UFO experience is every bit as significant as the social and psychological ones. Unless we accept that both exist and both must be incorporated into our solution, we may as well forget trying to work out what is going on.

We find this again from Arthur Koestler, when he looked at the problem with a philosopher's eyes. In 1978 he suggested, after studying the data, that UFOs were a product of our 'sickness' as a human race. It coincided with our rush to destroy ourselves through nuclear war (the truth behind the Satan legend is buried within ourselves). This was why the messages of alien contacts so often involve entities who knew we were destroying our own world. However, possibly there was a deeper reality behind the stories, generated through our perception of something else 'beyond human'.

Idle speculation perhaps. But the book was called *Janus* (after the two-faced god, chosen to reflect our sick and healthy sides). Almost exactly as it was released a family in Oxfordshire had a UFO encounter, lost time, were put under hypnosis by a Gloucester practitioner and a Birmingham University lecturer and from this an amazing 'memory' poured out. This epic case was later compiled into book form.[87] I spoke to the witnesses. They *were* sincere.

The aliens in this encounter claimed that they were once of earth and were returning to live here and to warn us, after having destroyed their own planet through nuclear mishaps and pollution. The symbolism is clear — especially when we learn that the alien moon which triggered the destruction was called Saton and the planet from whence they had fled like interstellar refugees was Janos.

If nothing else suggests that part of the UFO phenomen emerges from ourselves, then surely this incredibly appropriate case must do.

5.

Ether Monsters

Anyone captured by fairies or placed under a spell loses all sense of time.

J.C. Cooper, folklore researcher

A friend of my mother, with the delightful name of Blodwyn, told me about a frightening experience which happened to her long ago in the mid twenties.

She was looking after the feeding of some dairy cattle at a village beside the Wyre Forest, near Bewdley, Worcestershire. In order to collect some water she had to go into an old cave hollowed out of the hillside, which had a tradition of being used for religious ceremonies for many years. An old altar stone still remained inside.

Suddenly Blodwyn was overcome by a horrible sensation. A force more powerful than she had ever known grabbed hold of the young girl and seemed to tug at her throat. She felt the air being squeezed out of her windpipe and struggled desperately to break free. Finally she did so, and plunged out into the countryside, gulping down the fresh air.

When she reported her horrific encounter to the farmer he explained that local legend put the cave as fifteenth century. Allegedly a hermit had run away with a young girl, but the girl escaped in desperation and tried to return to her family. During the pursuit the girl had drowned. Her father or husband (it was not clear which) had chased the hermit and found him hiding out in the cave. here he had strangled the kidnapper to death.

Blodwyn explained that she was a sensitive person. She often knows intuitively what people are up to and gets a 'gut feeling' about the friendliness of an individual or a place. She had not connected this sensitivity with her experience in the hillside cave, which had baffled her throughout her life. But to me the solution seems obvious.

She somehow has the ability to 'read' emotions, just like blind people can read braille and decode a message. The raw emotion of that terrible life and death battle fought out within the confines of the cave had somehow imprinted itself across time and was still there to be picked up.

It is also worth noting that researchers Janet and Colin Bord have discovered a sighting of a 'phantom black dog' with huge glowing eyes that manifested in this same location in 1943.[88]

But why does this not happen all the time, with everyone who enters the area, or with every location that is the scene of such turmoil? It would appear to imply a need for a combination of the right person (in the right state of consciousness?) in the right place (an area somehow able to 'record'?) and possibly at the right time.

It is not always a mystical location like the cave. Quite frequently it happens in the mundane surroundings of the bedroom.

Jamil Mapindi* contacted me from Malaysia to show that such cases cross cultural boundaries. In 1981 he was staying alone in a house in Kuala Lumpur. He reports: 'One night, in the eary hours of the morning, I was awakened feeling the presence of something in my bedroom. I was laying on my right side and felt (it) at the foot of my bed behind me.'

He comments that he *knows* he was awake. In fact the experience 'pulled me out of sleep'. He felt an overwhelming 'evil' about it and 'my body was literally frozen'. He simply could not move. 'I felt terror; sheer, unbelievable terror. I did not think it was possible to be so afraid. In my head I heard a voice (it was not mine — I know what I sound like when I am thinking) . . . It said "Do not turn around", repeated several times.'

Despite not believing in God (and, he says, to his embarrassment), he found himself silently thinking: 'Please, God, help me.' Then the thing just went, but time had lost its meaning. 'It seemed hours, but it could not have been.'

The Oz factor, which I have mentioned several times in the book so far, is something that occurs in case after case, no matter what the type of paranormal experience. It is found in apparition cases, UFO encounters, time slips into the past and future, out of body states etc. I am certain it is a vital clue.[89]

Here the classic symptoms that recur in many Oz factor situations are the paralysis, the sensation within the mind, 'knowing' an experience is occurring, even when not being witnessed in a normal sensory manner, and the time suspension that affects the percipient. Other common attributes are an acute buzzing/humming noise 'within' the head and an electric skin-tingling sensation. The impression that 'all outside sounds have disappeared' often accompanies the experience when it takes place in an external environment, although this is less easy to recognize in the quiet of an early morning bedroom.

Overall the witness reports a feeling of 'reality' but with a curious aura. Common attempts to put this into words are 'it was as if I were in two worlds at once' . . . 'I felt awake and asleep at the same time' . . . 'I knew it was real but that nobody else around me was aware of this.'

However, Jamil's experience was not yet over. Half an hour later, quite unable to get back to sleep, he just 'knew' something else was about to occur when 'a cloud-like substance appeared on the built-in cupboards that were against the wall facing the foot of the bed. This then materialized into the figure of a woman.'

Jamil was so scared that he leapt out of bed and switched on the light. There was nothing there; although the room was icy cold.

He points out that since he was a small child he has had a history of undergoing psychic experiences and that five days after his night of terror, just as he had worked himself up to telling a friend, there was a sudden enormous bang. Rushing outside he found that all the windows on his car (front, back and sides) had shattered, sprinkling fine crushed glass particles *within* the car. It would seem that the only thing that might have caused such an implosion was a rapid drop in the air pressure inside the vehicle. This would then cause the outside air to force its way in through the windows.

As such stories imply it is often something about the person who faces the experience which is most important. But that is not always the case: sometimes there can be a more specific focal point.

Early in 1972 Dr Anne Ross, a Celtic scholar and archaeologist, was asked to examine some tiny stones just an inch or two across. They had carved into them crude faces with large crescent eyes. These had apparently been dug up from the garden of a council house in Hexham, Northumberland, one February afternoon by two of the children who lived there.

Dr Ross reports that she instantly disliked the stones but presumably knew that the family who discovered them wanted to get rid of them because they were 'cursed'. Their feeling was based on a few weeks of strange happenings when the heads had been inside their house and included typical poltergeist stories of objects moving about and suddenly breaking, glass shattering into tiny fragments and strange glows manifesting out of nowhere (sounds familiar?)

Even the next door neighbour, who spent a night sleeping in the children's room because of illness, claims she woke up to see a terrible shape 'half human and half sheep' and with claw-like hands. This materialized by the bed and then loped out. She screamed the house down and was so terrified the council had no option but to rapidly rehouse her.

As you can see there were plenty of things to un-nerve Dr Ross when she was given the stones. However, she tells of what occurred two nights after receiving them: 'I woke up suddenly at 2 a.m., deeply frightened and very cold. I looked towards the door and by the corridor light glimpsed a tall figure slipping out of the room.' She described it as 'part animal, part man' and says she felt a strange compulsion to follow it.[90]

She later told mystery researcher Paul Screeton, and the BBC, that 'a sort of dreadful atmosphere' soaked the room. She also said she thought the upper half of the figure more like a wolf than a sheep. Several days later, Dr Ross and her husband arrived home to find their teenage daughter Bernice in a state of shock. Whilst she knew nothing of her mother's nightmare experience, the girl had just entered the door when what she termed a 'werewolf' crashed noisily down the stairs, leapt over her head and banister rail and thudded into the music room. Here it vanished completely.

Several more manifestations of this thing occurred. It was said to be completely real and in no sense 'ghostly'. Of course, the Ross family soon got rid of the heads and nobody seems to know what happened to them after that.

Dr Ross was insistent that they were typical of Celtic carvings from the first or second century, used to ward off evil spirits. Although the stone could not be properly dated, a surprise announcement came after the story broke. Former resident of the infamous council house, Desmond Craigie, said that the stones were made by *him* in 1956. He had just been producing them as dolls for his daughter. He showed other similar heads he had made to prove his point. And later analysis in laboratories at Newcastle-upon-Tyne seemed to prove that they could not be very old.

Dr Ross continued to be baffled, because the heads which had been dug up were so identical with the really ancient carvings that litter the region. She pointed out that if Mr Craigie *did* make them, it was an amazing coincidence.

Furthermore, we have the tricky problem of what caused the various apparitions. Possibly Mr Craigie had the Celtic stone heads in mind when he made the ornaments, but could this thought, plus the act of burial, be enough to impress the strong mental image that could be 'read'?

Some interesting points to bear in mind are the name of the town where the stones were discovered — 'Hex' (i.e. a spell or curse) 'ham' (village). Another of our mysterious coincidences. We should also note the physical description of the rock containing the carvings: it was literally studded with rich quartz crystals — the sort of crystals the aliens gave Edwin in Sussex, the type of electric-signal generating mineral that paranormal researchers are now persuaded may cause the strange radiation effects that instruments frequently turn up at ancient stone-circle sites. [91]

Evidently there is more to this strange case than is at first apparent. It is all the more baffling when we look at the parallels drawn by David Clarke, long-time UFO investigator and now student of archaeology at Sheffield University. He lives in 'Brigantia', the ancient kingdom where the Celts thrived, and has been fascinated by the way their 'old gods' fit so remarkably with the modern stories we now presume to be 'space gods'.

In particular he shows how the stone-head carvings depict a flat face with large cat-like eyes and triangular chin that is incredibly similar to the most familiar sort of 'UFO entity' (the little grey man of American UFO abduction lore). Look at the cover of Whitley Strieber's book *Communion* and see the face that was plastered all over bus-shelters and advertising hoardings during 1988 to promote his Arrow paperback edition; it is the face of an alien (offered without explanation on the poster or book cover) which Strieber says he met in his bedroom in December 1986. It is also the face of the Celtic gods on these stone carvings.[92]

David Clarke further notes the predominance of the 'three' in Celtic mythology. The heads are often triple-sided, for instance. Yet the modern UFO story is literally packed with imagery of the three and triangles. Clarke cites some in his article. Strieber found others. We've already met one case with a triangle of three lights seen by a journalist over Lancashire. This is by no means the only one. The 'three' symbology is very clear.[93]

The strangest encounter that I have had, which might possibly be of supernatural origin, came whilst I was researching a book some years ago. It was the story of a young girl who had claimed magical visits from other beings (with facial features of the Celtic gods). Later she reported out-of-body trips to a bright, colourful land that was filled with exotic flora and fauna, far more like fairyland than the inside of any UFO.[94]

In my experience I was with my boyfriend on a gruelling motorcycle ride. We had set off in the early hours of 6 September 1980 to ride hundreds of miles south. After staying at our destination for a few hours we set off straight back to Cheshire. By 9.15 p.m. we were thoroughly exhausted but with still many more miles and hours of riding ahead of us. It demands far more concentration to stay on a powerful motorcycle than to drive a car where one can (although it is hardly advisable!) lie back and rest. Do that on a motorcycle and you are rather likely to fall off!

Briefly we saw three brilliant white lights appear above a hill to the south and line up into a triangle. Or rather I did. At the first opportunity we stopped to discuss it. My boyfriend had only seen one light (although of course he had to keep his eyes on the road so had a much more fleeting view). We placed the location on the map and it turned out to be right above the Avebury stone circle in Wiltshire. At the time we had no idea we were even close to this ancient monument of the Celtic era.

I know what I saw that night. It was a completely 'real' experience. My scepticism told me that it must have a simple explanation (e.g. parachute flares). But I put the case into the hands of responsible local UFO investigators and they could not find any solution. Also, we were on a busy motorway (which is why we could not stop) so the question remains as to why nobody else saw, or at least reported, the quite spectacular phenomenon.

I must say it has crossed my mind that being in such highly unusual circumstances it is possible that an altered state of consciousness caused us to visualize something out of the ordinary.

Since 1980 I have compiled accounts of dozens of similar cases. The Pennine Hills, for example, have generated a whole splurge of reports involving numerous independent witnesses. I have no doubt they are completely unaware of the pattern which they seem to be fulfilling. Yet they describe again and again (to me and many other investigators) a disc-like object with either three lights or, more often, three 'bumps' inset into the base in the form of a triangle. There are too many of these cases for it to be coincidence, or copying, particularly because most of them have never been made public and are little known even within the UFO community.

The most puzzling features of these cases are: the isolation factor (i.e. only one witness or a small group of people gathered together experience what takes place, even if they are surrounded by tens of thousands of people in the immediate vicinity); the Oz factor also rears its head, with peculiar changes in the witness behaviour and sensations of stillness and calm being widely recalled. There is clearly something of fundamental significance about this triangle experience.[95]

Of course, you may already see a possible connection between travelling in a tired frame of mind on a long monotonous journey and being in a semi-sleeping state in a bedroom. Both involve 'idling' states of consciousness. Is this why these 'bedroom visitor' experiences are so prevelant?

The force reported during these bedroom visitor encounters

is not always regarded by the witness as evil. It may be a neutral energy that is interpreted differently, according to personality or viewpoint.

A lady named Mrs Harrison* wrote to me from the Kings Cross area of Sydney in Australia. She offers a moving and very honest description of her struggle with alcoholism and the mysterious power that helped her through.

She explains that when thoroughly down and out and lost in a stupor she not infrequently heard a 'voice' inside her head that would direct her towards an unexpected lift. She then reports how at the bottom of this nightmare: 'My consciousness changed. I seemed to be in another dimension. I sat quietly on the bed and something took hold of my mind. I felt wonderful peace and calm. Everything slowed down. My girlfriend came into the room and later told me I seemed preoccupied.'

On other occasions the 'voice' has enabled her to locate objects and she believes it can be summoned by prayer or concentration. She recounts a time when it came to her in bed. It was 'a presence . . . all I can describe it as is "liquid love". It was overpowering, yet benevolent and compassionate.'

The most dramatic rescue operation came when her sensitivity, or whatever it was, prevented her from going straight into her house through the door one night. It was ajar, which she knew was odd, and instead of grabbing the handle and entering, as one would normally do, she pushed it open with her foot. The room was ransacked and the culprits, in an unbelievably inhuman act, had connected the door knob to the mains socket. Had she tried to open the door in the normal way she would have been killed.

Mrs Harrison regards this 'force' as the love of Christ, and I would not wish to challenge her religious views. But it is worth noting how the Oz factor sensations she describes (i.e. time slowing down) seem to link it in closely with other bedroom-visitor experiences that we have met.

Interpreting the force as a Christian spirit may in the end be little different from other people giving the same source and origin that makes sense to them, be it in a land beyond death or outer space, although I recognize that this statement could sound like heresy.

Paul from the West Midlands wrote to tell me about his bedroom visitors, mostly experienced as a young child. Usually they involved a yellowish face hovering over him, to which he seemed attracted like a magnet. As he was drawn towards the apparition he felt a vibration, there was a whining in his ears and he lost consciousness. He says that the face seemed as if it was extracted from a child's comic book. It was not exactly like any character he knew; it just had a 'flat' feel and was neither good nor evil, he concluded. Only his fear made it seem bad.

The experiences stopped when the family moved house, but he has still had visual episodes elsewhere. At a time when he was in a difficult reltionship with his mother he started to awake to the sound of marching feet, with voices rhythmically repeating 'hate her — hate her'. Once or twice he says that he 'saw' hooded figures outside.

More recently still he was 'between slumber and wakefulness' — a state of consciousness during which odd visional experiences can often occur. He saw 'what looked like a wizard in flowing robes with a sword raised above his head, held in his left hand. I saw him as I would an object that had been emitting light, and which had then gone out.'

Paul notes that this wizard 'was not just a product of my mind — the image was too strong for that'. Yet he does think he knows its source. At the time when these manifestations occurred he had been playing a computer game about wizards during waking hours.

So here we see a person with excellent ability for creating visual images. In the bedroom at night, when in an altered state of consciousness, various extremely vivid figures are 'conjured' up to 'haunt' him. They are very realistic, but fortunately he has sufficient caution and intelligence to question their status and not merely accept them as 'spectres'.

I am sure you can see how these figures might in other circumstances be considered spirit beings, alien entities, ghosts or evil forces. You may choose any one of the four, according to your tastes, belief systems or the current cultural vogue.

Take for instance this story. It happened to a young woman, whom I shall just call Frances, in January 1978. At the time she was separated from her husband and living with her young baby atop flats near Gateshead in Tyne and Wear — in fact exactly the same part of Tyneside where the 'little figures' leaping about over haystacks were reported previously (see page 120).

Frances awoke in the early hours with a high-pitched buzzing noise that 'seemed to be coming from inside my head'. She likened the tingling vibrations to an electric shock. After this happened several nights in succession she got the impression that something was trying to wake her up: 'I felt my head would burst if I didn't open my eyes.'

By this point she was sleeping on the couch, terrified of the bedroom. But that did not help much. Nor did leaving the light switched on. Then suddenly someone took hold of her hand. Frances says: 'I thought I was dreaming, because the whole thing seemed to have a dreamy atmosphere.' Yet her mind was thinking rationally. She looked over at the clock and saw it was 3.50 a.m. Being unable to bring herself to look at the person holding her hand, all she saw was the arm. It was covered in a bluish 'suit' and a glow lit up her own hand. She could see through it as if it were an X-ray photo!

Still in a 'trance', she says that she took her hand away. The glow persisted for a few more seconds, then faded. Suddenly, time 'jumped'. Looking at the clock she saw that several minutes had passed and there was no recollection of what took place inbetween. The buzzing and the figure had gone. She got out of bed, made some tea to calm her nerves and had the sense to write all of this down so as to remember it as accurately as possible whilst she could still do so. [96]

To me the most fascinating aspect of this story is not the complete sincerity of Frances and the way she offered no framework or explanation for this figure. Nor is it again the clear report of the Oz factor or the link with the Felling 'elves' dancing on the haystack. It was the fact that between 1976 and 1979 *two* more cases took place (with no real publicity), both in this small region where coal mining, pits and fault lines are scattered about — something we should bear in mind.

The first occurred on 3 September 1976 in a mining area near a piece of waste ground where building work was going on. An elderly lady and her teenage niece allegedly came upon a small oval object with an orange dome on top. They felt 'hypnotically attracted' towards it. As they walked across the ground, the Oz factor took hold. All sounds vanished, time 'stood still' (afterwards a watch was running slow as if it had stopped for ten minutes). Standing by the object the woman saw two small creatures, described as living 'dolls' with long, white hair and huge eyes. They seemed frightened and the woman backed away, suddenly finding that the environmental sounds had returned to normal. The thing left amidst a large 'humming' noise.[97]

The other case was exactly three years later, during the period late August to early September 1979. Indeed the main event was on the precise three-year anniversary of 3 September. Carol, aged 22, was the main percipient, in a very similar situation to Frances — bringing up a three-year-old daughter with her husband frequently away on night shift.

To cut a very long story short, Carol was besieged by buzzing noises, tingling sensations and paralysis — the familiar bedroom visitor sensations. Small discs of light would materialize through her window and fly about the room. Most family members endured something. Finally, on the fateful night of September 3, at 4 a.m., a little disc 'landed' in the corner of her bedroom. She tried to scream but was unable to do so and as the usual 'floating' sensation took hold, with its tingles and paralysis, a group of tiny human-like figures came towards her bed. They were two to three feet tall, had 'pale' and 'effeminate' faces (although they seemed male) and large eyes. They took great interest in her spectacles beside the bed and (without speaking) one of them 'said': 'She is just like any other earthling,' followed by a series of clicking noises.

John Watson, who investigated the case, was totally baffled. The terror was certainly real. When he was there the entire family were sleeping in one single room as the only way of reassuring themselves that the visitors would not return.[98]

Surely the extremely consistent patterns that we find in these cases is of great importance. Can we really explain them in purely psychological terms, waving away such bizarre experiences as nothing but hallucinations?

If we knew why this one small part of north-east England has generated four encounters with these unusual figures, showing such consistent patterns, despite little likelihood that any witness knew of the other cases, then we might understand the essence of this phenomenon.

Notice how we call the beings 'elves' when dancing on haystacks, 'aliens' when apparently beside a landed UFO, 'elementals' when floating about bedrooms alongside balls of light, and 'ghost' when simply there on its own by the foot of a bed. But surely the name we give is simply a convenient way to explain the apparition to ourselves. It may have no more substance behind it than that; although, obviously, *some* truth has to lie behind these stories.

In my travels I have come across many cases where similar circumstances have led to an encounter with some type of entity. The precise form the entity takes does vary, but that is far less significant than the background to the report. For instance, here is a quick summary of a few cases. Look at the common denominators.

In Dar-es-Salaam, Africa, in about 1950, a young girl (then aged five) woke at 3 a.m. to find a strange noise in the bedroom (like a distant grinding, vibrating humming engine that seemed to be *above* the house). Then she 'felt I was being watched — you know when you can stare at the back of someone's head and they immediately turn to look at you'. At the foot of the bed was 'the ugliest thing I had ever seen': a tiny person about two or three feet tall with 'huge eyes . . . a pale face, no mouth, just a trace of lips, and a pointed (triangular) chin that thinned from the eyes downward'. It started to move towards her and she screamed. Her father rushed in but found nothing. As she says: 'I knew I wasn't dreaming. No nightmare has ever stayed so vividly with me.' After the experience she started to get pains in the head and neck 'like tightening bands' and from her teens onward she suffered from powerful migraines and unexpected, sudden body 'twitches'.

In August 1961 in Alberta, Canada, John Brent Musgrave reports on a case reported to him in his role as a UFO investigator. A young man awoke at about 3.30 a.m. to find himself totally paralysed but strangely calm. At the foot of the bed were two figures, just four feet tall, and with a dome-shaped 'bubble' on their heads. They floated around 'communicating' (into his mind) saying they would see him again and then adding: 'I think he's waking up on us — we'd better go'. There was a 'hissing' and suddenly the man was free of the spell he had been under. He leapt up out of bed, as did his wife beside him. She claimed that she had also been 'in a trance' and had seen the figures. A bluish glow in the sky around the house was also witnessed by outsiders, allegedly rising slowly into the air.[99]

A few years after this in Britain two cases reached me as part of a ghost survey. In one, the witness, who lived in an ordinary house in Birmingham, was awoken in the middle of the night by a strange 'feeling', and then saw a glowing figure emerging from the wall at the point where the wardrobe was. The occupants knew the house had been built on the site of an old airfield and the figure was said to look like a World War Two airman. It floated forwards a little and then vanished.

Even more extraordinary was the case which was reported to me when I was doing a regular series of programmes for Radio City on Merseyside. It happened in an old terraced house at Bootle, just north of Liverpool. In the sixties the building still had an outside toilet and when a member of the family awoke in the middle of the night, no matter how sleepy, he or she was forced to tramp down the stairs and out to his rather primitive facility. On one occasion the toilet was 'occupied', but not by any member of the family. The unfortunate late night visitor found a glowing form inside the little outhouse which, as far as he could see, looked remarkably akin to some kind of scantily-clad primitive tribesman: 'It was just like a Zulu Warrior'. But it vanished before anybody could confront it.

On other occasions I have heard similar stories where the late night apparition has been 'seen' as a giant frog and a naked 'streaker' bolting through the bedroom!

Consistently in these cases we have the figure being seen shortly after waking, i.e. within an altered state of consciousness. Yet there are times when the vision is 'shared' by others in the immediate vicinity, suggesting it is not just an image inside the mind. How the 'glow' is interpreted varies widely, and there are hints that this might depend upon personal knowledge. If you know your house was built on the site of an airfield, what is more natural than to treat your visitor as the ghost of a flier? If you live in a region where UFOs are the aviators, then this offers a good hook for the experience. Where the more bizarre forms come from is an interesting question, but it probably still fits the basic pattern.

Of further interest are the details we note when these cases are studied in more depth: the Oz factor, the strange noises, the paralysis, the subjective elements to counteract apparent reality (e.g. the voices inside the head and 'feelings' that initiate the encounter). And, possibly most crucial, the migraine, headband pains and other after-effects which have cropped up in several cases. Some UFO researchers claim that they are the product of the 'aliens' establishing mental contact with the witness, but to me they suggest that the experience itself depends upon something happening *within* the brains of those who fall victim to such things.

But if this is anything like what is taking place, do we have any examples of what researcher Hilary Evans calls a 'grafting' process? Cases where the phenomenon at the root of the encounter is seen as somehow amorphous, *before* being turned into something more exotic?

Take the story related to me by Olive Dewhurst-Maddock from Cumbria. It was May 1985 (the 28th or 29th) and she was with her husband and friends on the slopes of a farm at Myddfai in rural west Wales. They had watched the sun set over the Towy Valley and at 7.30 p.m. were observing clouds build up after a warm day. There then followed an event about which Olive asked me: 'Could this be blind chance or was there more to it?'

The clouds started to form into the shape of a UFO. Hanging in the air above the Brecon Beacons it was an amazing spectacle: a dome on top, a row of portholes around the rim and rays of light being projected from the base, presumably sunlight, although reminiscent of searchlight beams. Olive watched for several minutes and it seemed to stay in one place. She felt a kind of 'oneness' and remained gazing up in stillness and silence. As she puts it: 'I felt astounded, but not surprised. It seemed inevitable and familiar.' Later she commented on her strange decision not to bring it to the atention of the others (and they seem not to have 'seen' it). 'The whole thing was unremarkable, in an unaccountable way . . . At no time did I think of the shape as anything more than an extraordinary cloud . . . I felt it was "natural", but significant.'

The phenomenon vanished by 'dissolving' apparently more quickly than ordinary clouds would do. Superficially we have nothing but a coincidentally-shaped cloud. Yet the strange state of consciousness which Olive displayed has all the features we have seen in the Oz factor and hints at deeper things. Did she 'manufacture' the UFO from the cloud in some truly fantastic way? Especially as we note that she was personally interested in the subject and had read books on the theme.

David Clarke investigated another interesting case from a house at Nether Edge, South Yorkshire. Essentially this sounds like a ghost or poltergeist. But if it had occurred *outside*, rather than *inside* a building, there is no doubt that it would be viewed as a UFO.

The phenomenon was a 'blob' of roughly human size but which altered shape and seemed to be made up of fine 'speckly' particles, like dust motes catching the sunlight, or vaporous cigar smoke. It normally appeared in the bedroom but on one occasion the lady of the house walked *through* it before she realized it was there. On doing so she felt 'cold', but there was no apparent resistance. However, there had also been inexplicable electrical failures in the building and someone with fine hairs on her arm felt these standing on end, clearly implying an electrostatic field was present.

Indeed, perhaps the 'blob' was created from the fine dust particles in the house somehow being brought together in the attraction of a localized electric field. If so, what caused the field and why was the shape perceived as a kind of 'entity'? Did the witness somehow manipulate the particles like a child might rearrange building blocks to form the shape of something which appealed to him or her subconsciously? Is this the same process that juggled particles of water vapour to mould a cloud into a UFO?

It is worth noting that in both these cases the witnesses were 'artistic'. Olive Dewhurst-Maddock is a professional musician. The housewife who saw the blob in the Sheffield semi (far more often than other family members), has undergone repeated out of body experiences and vivid dreams where she flies through a window and seems to be awake. She has also seen a more traditional ghost, a UFO and had frequent problems with mysterious interference on the telephone.[100]

Again we see reason to suspect that certain types of people may be 'creating' these ethereal entity forms and that *they* might be responsible for the form that these figures adopt. Perhaps they build them up from something real, if intangible, by a process taking place *within* the mind.

There are many more similar cases which seem to show that entities can be built into something that is convincing to the witness. This process appears to be more than just 'reading' a shape into a blob, rather like someone visiting a psychiatrist might see meaningful images in an ink blot. We have already seen how in the case of the engineer at Risley, Cheshire, a white blob (entity) that was non-material (i.e. it walked straight through a security fence) was certainly connected with a real electrical energy field (which destroyed his radio set with an enormous power surge and possibly brought about his untimely death).

At Press Heath in Shropshire on 28 February 1981 three men were hunting rabbits in early hours of the morning on the grounds of a disused prisoner of war camp, when a white glow floated towards them 'bobbing up and down like a cork'. Its face was oval and only two large eyes were visible. The form pulsed greenish yellow and then red. *All* of them saw it. One stood paralysed and could not move. The second dropped all his gear and fled. However, the third brave soul threw a stone at the thing. It passed right through the shape and the figure 'disappeared' just like it was 'a slide being projected'.

Here is another excellent illustration of this process in operation. It was described by Frank Earp who was a child of 15 at the time (1966), playing with two friends beside a disused canal in Wollaton near Nottingham. They were interested in the supernatural and looking for UFOs.

At dusk a misty vapour rose from the watercourse and formed a cloud about the size of a dodgem car. Nothing odd about that — marsh gas, will o'the wisp, or any similar phenomenon might be thought to blame. But a doughnut-shaped 'blob' was now heading in their direction. Not surprisingly they set off into a trot. A peculiar glow was emerging from within the cloud.

Once near enough to the safety of the houses Frank turned to confront the thing. He was just 20 feet away. It was a six-foot tall 'furry' creature, not unlike a sasquatch, with claw-like hands gripping two red 'lights'. Weirdest of all, the legs appeared to fade away into nothingness. Frank and one of his friends ran for home. The third boy (who was stood within touching distance of the monster) called after them in bemused fashion. It later turned out that he had only seen the cloud, not the entity which his friends had detected. [101]

Perhaps this same mechanism has been going on for centuries and clouds and other radiating energy sources have turned into entities that were relevant to the time in question. We only have to look at some reports of fairy sightings to see the remarkable comparison with what we are now discovering.

A famous legend from Cornwall concerns Anne Jefferies. Historian Robert Hunt reports in his *Popular Romances of the West of England* that in 1645 she was in the garden of her employers when the teenage girl felt a whirling sensation and a floating dizziness and lost consciousness just as she was approached by two small beings (fairies).

Anne regained her senses in 'fairyland', or rather a colourful flower-filled place which contained many of these strange beings. They were apparently very interested in human sexual reproduction but Anne was not retained (although the idea that she did not remember everything seems implicit in the tale). Her return was marked by the same floating sensation and blackout accompanied by a sound described as 'a thousand flies buzzing about her'. After this she developed a reputation as a psychic and healer and stopped eating various sorts of food.

There is not the slightest doubt how this story would be reported by a tabloid newspaper nowadays. Anne would have been 'abducted' by aliens and she would immediately be subjected to hypnosis and some sort of 'memory' would emerge for what else happened.

What this story (and plenty of others like it) has in common with modern UFO abductions appears to be so precise that it must mean we are dealing with the same phenomemon, interpreted differently according to the times.

Also we find in Anne Jefferies' story two more vital clues. Firstly, she was carried back into the house semi-conscious and was *still* having her vision at this point. Indeed, when she came around completely, some minutes later, she reported that the fairies had just left (via the window); although nobody in the house saw them and they were evidently part only of her inner-world reality.

Exactly the same situation has occurred in several UFO cases.

A young girl from Wales, like Anne Jefferies in many respects, also floated into a bright land, experiencing identical sensations. Whilst she was 'away' her mother chanced to enter the room and found her prone on the bed in a deep 'trance-like' state. The girl's condition was considered sufficiently unusual for her mother to check again soon afterwards to ensure that her daughter was now sleeping normally.[102]

The second vital clue in the Anne Jefferies story is that when found in the garden after her fairy abduction her body was jerking about and she was having 'convulsions'. This sounds very much as if she were undergoing an epileptic attack.

Epilepsy is a disorder of the brain chemistry and an estimated 300,000 people in Britain alone suffer from it (i.e. one in every 200). There are no clearly understood causes. In fact epilepsy is often a symptom of another disorder, rather than a disease in its own right.

Anyone is a potential victim and not infrequently people do not know they suffer unless they have a brain scan. In fact occasional epileptic attacks are even more common and it is believed that 1 in 20 people will have a brief period of epilepsy at some point in their lives.

Two medical writers on the problem said: 'We are all "epileptics", for any one of us can suffer a seizure if the appropriate circumstances arise.'[103] Problems start when chemical changes affect the sequence of electrical firing of neurons in the brain, so that these get out of step. Trigger factors are as diverse as a brain tumour, intense fear, electric shock and bright pulsating lights flashing in a way that 'synchronizes' with the brain. Low blood-sugar is another factor, and this is why some people often suffer attacks only at night (when the blood sugar is at a reduced level).

It should be obvious that several of these triggers could occur during monster experiences. Are we seeing evidence that unexpected epileptic attacks are somehow associated with these encounters?

Common after-effects of an epileptic attack are brief periods of paralysis, headache or tight-band sensations round the head and a period of deep sleep. Indeed sometimes an epileptic seizure leads only to a partial loss of consciousness and the sufferer wanders around like a sleep-walker, still aware of his surroundings on one level but possibly experiencing a 'dream journey' at the same time.

Regular sufferers also note that attacks can sometimes be sensed before they happen. They involve an 'aura', or vague feeling of unease. Unexpected smells and other sensory distortions can also occur through the chemical alterations in the brain affecting our perception systems.

I doubt if I need to point out just how many of these things match up with features of the monster stories that we have met throughout this book.

Migraine sufferers are even more numerous and there are many similarities here: the aura that warns of an attack; some of the triggers (blood-sugar changes, stress and bright lights); and several of the symptoms (e.g. the tight-band pain in the head). I have noticed that many witnesses to monster experiences profess to being regular migraine victims. It could be that this is another highly important discovery.

If we return to stories about fairies in our hunt for more clues, we can find plenty. Every culture seems to have its own long traditions of 'little people', 'elementals' and 'spirit beings'. For instance, in the Baltic countries it was said that to enter 'fairyland' one had to stand on a crystal point within a hill. Irish tales of little folk also speak of the importance of crystal in their world. In Scandinavia they say that one reaches this other world by climbing up a crystal mountain.

We have seen in our search through case histories that crystals (especially quartz) feature quite often, as indeed do hills. We suspect a more mundane scientific explanation connected with the electricity that these crystals under stress can generate. But it is fascinating to find that global tradition links them in with fairy encounters.

Another similarity is with the effects on time. In fairyland this has always been said to be distorted and tales of the 'Rip van Winkle' type are very common; a person enters a trance and goes to another world, then returns (often years later) to be amazed at how the lost years have vanished from his memory.[104]

The Oz factor and UFO abduction are just a modern update on this theme, with their time suspension and 'missing time' elements.

In a collection of fairy lore going back as far as 1691, Robert Kirk described some of their now very familiar attributes. Fairies like to protect their secrecy and try to prevent people talking about their existence. If necessary they abduct witnesses and can tamper with their minds. They change shape, but essentially have bodies that are made out of 'solidified air'. Yet they easily adapt to the environment they live in and take on the form of the local inhabitants, although smaller in stature. They are basically good but do have a tendency to tell lies and pretend to be things they are not. The best time to see them is at dusk or around midnight.[105]

I expect some of this will ring a few bells with most readers.

Another more recent survey of fairy legends adds even further to the parallels. Here we learn that fairies are not the tiny inch-high creatures that childrens' story books allege. Their normal height in the real encounters was similar to that of a child aged about four. We also hear that they usually claimed the need to kidnap people because of a desire to interbreed with humans. They often ask for help in some way (e.g. to borrow tools or carry out repairs) and in return they pay for these favours with gifts that seem on the surface to be rubbish but are in fact 'magic'. They are said to be able to float and to disappear at will.[106]

Of course, we might believe fairies are just ancient yarns created by imaginative people who did not have TV sets to keep themselves amused, in which case, there would be no modern cases of fairies (UFO entities sit well within the space age, but not elementals). However, fairies are *still* seen. Researcher Joe Cooper has collated over a dozen reports from modern Britain and they usually involve witnesses in a dreamy state of consciousness (e.g. idling by a river bank in summer) and those who are both visually creative or artistic in some way.

Two other cases on more public record are very illuminating. On 9 August 1977 at 1.30 a.m., Police Officer David Swift went to investigate a mysterious bank of fog or vapour on playing fields in Stonebridge Avenue, Hull. Here he discovered three figures that were dancing in the mist. They wore fairy-like clothing (e.g. jerkins) and had arms aloft as if holding something above their heads. As he set off towards them the whole ensemble just disappeared. (Again we see forms emerging out of an amorphous bank of vapour.)

The second case is even more ridiculous. This took place on 29 October 1979 when several young children (Andrew and Rosie Pearce, Angela Elliot and Patrick Olive) were walking home at dusk. Suddenly they heard tinkling sounds and saw a large group of little men (about two feet tall) with greenish casts and white beards apparently driving little cars all over an area of marsh. The creatures seemed to be upset by any lights.

Patrick fell in the swamp in his haste to get away, but the children seemed sincere in their stories. They informed their headmaster (not the sort of thing a hoaxing child is likely to do). This man, Robin Aldridge, later said: 'They really believe in what they saw.'

Two things were not mentioned about this case. One was that the area had a reputation for being 'haunted' by fairies. The other was the location in a park at Wollaton near Nottingham, the place where Frank Earp and his friends had a monster encounter thirteen years before.

So yet another consistent clue emerges — the repeat location, or as some researchers call it, the 'window' area. Nottinghamshire, like the north-east, is noted for its coalfields with many disused pits, quarries and fault-ridden rocks. Can this really be a coincidence?

6.

A Monster Menagerie

May the universe in some strange way be 'brought into being' by the participation of those who participate?

John Wheeler, physicist

It is time to take stock of where we stand. Then we can look towards science for answers to our questions.

Of course, scientists are not gods. They may not have the solution to our problems. But there has been far too much confrontation of late. Paranormal researchers treat science like the enemy and scientists often treat the paranormal as if it were nonsense, and dangerous nonsense at that.

Indeed, Dr J. Allen Hynek, certainly the nicest and one of the most brilliant men I have had the privilege of knowing, from his then almost unique position as *both* scientist and paranormal-ist, likened the handling of the topic by most of his peers to the carrying of 'a decaying rat' towards the nearest city dump.

Yet, as we will shortly come to realize, both physical and psychological science are now heading down converging paths, squeezing the pips from the ground in their midst. And, although many of them have failed to realize it, that middle ground has the word 'monster' painted all over it. For here is a worldwide experimental demonstration of their obtuse and hypothetical theories. The things they decry are ironically the very things they seek.

As for cryptozoologists, UFO researchers and other pheno-mena hunters, the fear seems to be that science will nip in and steal their thunder. They want to be the ones to say 'I told you so' and prove that the earth is being invaded by Martians. Subconsciously they may see a threat from solutions that demystify the mysterious, because once the paranormal becomes thoroughly normal they no longer face life as a 'hero' in a world of disbelievers. Explain these monsters and we will hear the hiss of air rapidly escaping from several thousand inflated egos. We may then see the hapless band of paranormalists trailing in the wake of the scientific masses, now suddenly chanting, 'well, we knew that all along'.

This is just human nature and quite understandable. However, if we are to find the truth (and I hope, like me, that is all you are looking for) we have to forego these battlelines and glean what we can from our case histories.

Too often when scientists or paranormalists say that they are searching for the 'truth', what they really mean is they are searching for confirmation of their beliefs. Of course, some theory is necessary as a starting-point for knowledge. But in this business we sink in the quicksands double-fast if we fail to demonstrate flexibility. We *must* follow where the evidence trail leads even if it is dragging us, screaming and kicking, away from all our fondest hopes and dreams.

So let us quickly survey the main points of interest emerging from our monster hunt.

Firstly, there are so many overlaps between most of these phenomena that we appear to be dealing with variations on a single theme.

Personally, I suspect that in one or two cases we *might* (and I stress the word might) have a real 'monster'. The most likely, in my opinion, is the Congo dinosaur, which could be an evolutionary cast-off that has survived 60 million years of isolation (and presumably developed along the way). Let me say that I would not be surprised to find acceptable proof in the not too distant future and I only hope that movies such as *King Kong* and *Godzilla* have got it wrong and we do not treat such a marvellous creature as a freak show.

However, for the vast majority of our monster stories, their physical reality seems much more open to question. Above all they represent a *reflective* phenomenon.

I have recently heard from Bert, a former air force radio

operator, who lives in New Zealand. He wanted to relate something that happened to his father-in-law long ago in 1924.

At the time he was a potter firing kilns at a small factory in a village in South Otago. It was about 6 a.m. As he emerged into the open air he saw an 'aircraft' flying low on the horizon. The object flew behind two hills and came out the other side, then passed behind a third and *never* came out. It simply disappeared. Whilst this was happening the strangest thing of all was the sudden stillness and silence — the ever faithful Oz factor. As the man said, in the country you notice the quiet when it comes. He asked around but nobody had seen this amazing sight. All he received for his pains were amused requests to tell them what sort of grog he had been drinking!

Clearly we see here many features of the kind of experience which happens to a witness out of the blue and yet which seems to take place for his eyes only, plus the evidence that it occurred in an altered state of consciousness where the outside sensory data was 'turned out' to be replaced by imagery from some *inner* source. We recognize this as the Oz factor, and it has been happening down through the ages.

Sixty-plus years on there is no doubt how the 'aircraft' would have been perceived now — as a spaceship with all the trimmings. But UFOs did not exist in 1924. We know from studies that have been carried out by many diligent researchers that there was a 'UFO' wave in 1896-7 in the USA and another the following decade in Britain, but that these UFOs were highly unusual, being seen as forms of *airship* which apparently never flew in any conventional sense.[107] In the thirties there were strange silent 'bi-planes' seen in similar circumstances and, just before the spaceships 'landed', in 1946, Scandinavia had a spate of ghostly rockets and missiles.

This Otago 'UFO' was the 1924 'rural villager' variety and was described as 'like an aeroplane, but instead of any wings this craft had what looked like a large windmill on the top'.

As we see, the phenomenon has the ability to appear in a form that is acceptable to the percipient. Precisely as the tales of fairies in the Middle Ages say the elementals were wont to do. We see this repeatedly, from the Ninja dwarfs who reflected their observers to the interaction between Gothic novels and 'real' encounters with 'Spring Heel Jack' and his ilk.

This leads us even further into the murky waters of synchronicity, i.e. the coming together of two seemingly unrelated events in an apparently meaningful way.

Author Ian *Watson* conjures up a novel about how the mind can 'invent' realistic UFOs, monsters and pterodactyls. At precisely the same time researcher Nigel *Watson* is investigating cases (in the same location where the writer set his novel). These have not been publicized but feature an identical character involved with 'real' UFOs, monsters and pterodactyls.

I have found this in a number of other cases.[108] There is a definite clue in this symbiotic link between fact and fiction. I believe it implies that *both* emerge from that part of the subconscious which is common to our species. It may be here where all sorts of primitive imagery lurks, such as behavioural defence mechanisms against dinosaurs inherited down the millenia from our mammalian ancestors who lived alongside the beasts.

For some reason, and at certain times, something can come from the depths of this 'ocean of images' and be used to formulate fiction or vivid 'real' experiences. It may only be a difference of degree and the personal talents or preferred mode of expression. In that sense Ian Watson was every bit as much a 'contactee' as the witness his namesake followed through.

There were more suggestions of this ocean of images when we saw the name games that were played. We only need look at some of the locations of these monster experiences which feature in the book: Angel Marshes, Devil's Garden, Mal-Graves Farm, Il-minster, Hex-ham. Possibly such places may occasionally earn their names because of strange events which have occurred there throughout history. Or is it that this universal ocean of images operates not on logic and deduction but — like the dream — through symbols and connectivity? We might then understand how a seemingly ridiculous coincidence could occur almost like a cosmic joke.

In one of my dreams I was caught in a flood. To escape I desperately needed a boat. But instead a grand piano floated by. I jumped on that and was rescued. When discussing this with a psychologist who studied dreams, I learnt that the symbology and pun-making elements are often strong and that my mind probably searched for a ship, thought of the P & O shipping line and phonetically turned this into a pi- an- o!

We appear to have a similar process going on in the world of the paranormal and that certainly offers direct evidence that the experience is occurring as some mental phenomenon.

Another important clue that crops up is that a monster encounter rarely stands in isolation in the life of the witness. Whilst they come from a cross-section of society, are undoubtedly sincere, and often of considerable intelligence (not the gullible dreamers that debunkers would wish them to be), witnesses are also in some way a 'special' group.

These people are often artistic in some sense. We frequently see them engaged in pursuits such as poetry, creative writing, art, pottery, etc. I have noticed that quite a number are in 'caring' professions (e.g. nursing). I suspect this is because such a career is a good expression of these people's unique abilities to take in and live with strong emotional expressions or visual images.

Evidence that witnesses to *monster reality* tend to be extremely gifted in a visually creative fashion. One woman in Virginia, USA, had an experience with lights and strange creatures and subsequently developed her marked musical and artistic talent. She also officially changed her name. Her beautiful portraits try to capture the flavour of her experiences and the phenomenon (*Judith Starchild*).

Repeatedly I have heard witnesses say that they 'cry' easily, or are suddenly overcome with depression or elation. The capacity to soak up emotions like a sponge may be what makes an individual a good psychic. I am reasonably certain it is what makes a good monster witness.

In the early days of our species there were 'storytellers' in every village. These were the people who kept the tribe amused and preserved its history. We saw hints that early man could have been more in touch with monsters, because the imagery more readily broke through into his consciousness. I suspect it also broke through to the very people who became the storytellers and that is why many myths and legends came to persist. Very probably the same process is going on today, but we call these people by names such as 'mediums' or 'clairvoyants'. And, of course, we give them far less respectability than they were afforded in another day and age.

As we head towards a crisis point in society (interestingly coincident with that metaphorical 'species puberty' we uncovered) then perhaps there are signals aplenty rushing at us from that ocean of images, producing waves of monster sightings as messages or warnings.

An 18-year-old wrote to me from Bahrain. He explains how since the age of five or six he remembers 'fairies' in the garden. One night he tells me: 'I woke up for no reason and put on my slippers, ran to the window and pulled back the curtains . . . then I saw the fairies. They were flying about and all I could relate them to was a cartoon. Then I woke up in the morning in my bed.' Naturally the youngster thought this was a dream, until over by the window he found his slippers and the curtains flapping open.

Around this time he also had regular flying sensations of an 'out of body' nature (stepping out onto the window ledge and floating away), but these were gradually replaced by precognitive dreams in which he saw many family events before they happened. Then, as the years went by, these in turn were superceded by UFO encounters of 'three stars' that were 'dancing'. On one night: 'I just couldn't believe it. They swooshed down from above and they were three domes with flat surfaces on the bottom, very silvery but also pale. They were in a triangular formation and they started to move around me . . . I ran like anything and called my parents out, but there was nothing there. I've tried to block this from my memory, because nobody believes me.'

The youth's 'real reason' for contacting me was because he was now regularly waking up 'at 3 o'clock at night, drained, like a blackout'. One specific occasion in late 1987 he awoke 'at 2 o'clock with a feeling of being pulled . . . I was paralysed and couldn't scream.' He knew that something had happened involving 'aliens', but did not know what.

As we can see, someone with a 'psychic track record' is very often at the heart of these encounters. They may build up over a lifetime from simpler to more complex forms, which hints strongly as to what these experiences might be. They evidently do not simply happen to anybody in the right place at the right time. The *person* at the focal point is significant.

Another discovery was that there do appear to be 'window areas' where monster sightings are more commonplace. The obvious deduction would be that Loch Ness, for example, is a window area because the monster lives there, so that is where people see it. Unfortunately, such logic is demolished when we recognize just how often other strange phenomena are mixed up in the pattern at the same location.

Look at the cases in the north-east of England around Gateshead, where a plague of 'little men' is occurring; or the fairy or sasquatch events in Wollaton near Nottingham; or the 'big cat' haunts in the Rossendale Valley and a disused quarry in Stacksteads (coincidentally, the small hill village where I was born and raised). Now instead of mountain lions the same rocky slopes are alive with UFOs said to be landing in that same quarry. Even as I write, in January and February 1989, more encounters have occurred leading UFO spotters on a quest to find the spaceships in the hills. And at Loch Ness itself there have been UFO encounters as well as monster sightings. One man took photographs of both, and another Nessie photographer demonstrated the Loch's 'psychic' nature by somehow evoking Nessie's appearance as well as that of a Cornish sea-monster.

What have all these places in common? The answer is mining areas, fault lines, rock quarries, and in the Ninja dwarf case, nearby sandstone outcrops, where a mysterious tremor seemed to terminate all activity.

Hills and rock faults were not the only consistencies we found amidst the cases. Again and again we found comparisons. For example: a sulphurous/ozone smell, evidence of electrostatic fields or electrical impedence, glowing eyes, humming/buzzing sounds (and the connections with epilepsy which might imply something going on within the electrical circuits of the brain), the floating and insubstantial nature of the entity, its imperviousness to attack or to bullets, an ability to vanish instantly even when cornered (e.g. the Jersey Devil trapped inside a barn), its shape-changing capacity and its ability to grow and develop into its monstrous form from mists, vapours, clouds and other amorphous blobs of light.

Then think about those photographs of these amoeba-like shapes: the Nessie picture which is either a monster or a swimming dog, according to how we look at it; the Rochdale policeman and his UFO or helmet (again depending on interpretation); and the Doc Shiels monster photographs which computer enhancement says are semitransparent, flat and two-dimensional.

Then there was the UFO-riding sasquatch from Sheffield, where the witness commented that what he saw was like a 'projection'; the rabbit hunters in Shropshire who saw the 'ghost' (or alien, or monster) which to them was akin to a 'projected slide'. And the monster chase in Nottingham where two witnesses saw 'bigfoot' but the youth closest to it only saw a vaporous cloud.

And, probably more significant than all of these, the photograph of the ape-man seen in Ohio which came out well, but only showed a great big blob of light.

I think this tells us that the monster itself may be based on something that emerges from that ocean of images common to the human race, and may partly owe its origin to the minds of certain people (those who are visually creative, who absorb emotions and have a psychic track record).

But there is more to it than that. There is a physical component as well. Something that is tangible and real, that may have electrical fields or emitted radiation associated with it and may look basically vaporous or resemble a glowing blob of light. Somehow this blob *becomes* our menagerie of monsters through a process that depends upon the witness to the experience. A form of pseudo-reality is *created* from an amorphous starting-point, around which myths, legends and mysteries congregate to form the equivalent of an expanding snowball rolling down a hill.

The sceptics are going to cry out at this point that what I am saying is that monsters are mere hallucinations. But I am not saying that at all. I am claiming that monsters may be an inter-mediary reality *between* solid, objective, physical matter, and dreamy, subjective, symbol-laden images — reality that is both real and unreal, physical and subjective, and solid and symbolic at the very same time.

Here is a remarkable case which seems to illustrate the point.

The witness, Roy Smith,* is a design engineer from Cheshire. He is highly artistic with a very refined technical drawing ability. In late October 1984 he awoke at 6 a.m. to find a strange dark figure at the foot of his bed. This was slight, frail and under five feet tall. It wore a skin-tight black uniform that was almost 'sprayed on' and which revealed most unusual facial features (chiefly a dramatically triangular chin). The figure radiated directly into his mind sensations of calmness and curiosity, and in a second experience some weeks later a feeling of timeless-ness — Oz factor indications that the witness was in an altered state of consciousness during these episodes.

Subsequently Roy had a whole series of strange incidents in-volving coincidences, premonitions, poltergeist effects around the house and curious electrical interferences. His computer screen also started to display intelligent messages on its own!

I was greatly impressed by this witness, who frequently ques-tioned the substance of his experience and performed many 'reality checks' upon it. In particular three points stood out which persuaded him that he was not merely experiencing an hallucination: first, it had three-dimensional structure (he saw it edge on and face on and there were shadow highlights cast upon it); second, as he moved to see its lower portions (hidden by the bedclothes) it vanished instantaneously ('the white of the wall behind it literally rushed in on me'); third, and most signifi-cant of all, the fact that Roy is short-sighted. Anything further than five feet from his retina is slightly out of focus. This entity displayed that fuzziness. He had to continually screw up and unscrew his eyes in order to see it sharply. As he told me: 'Surely an hallucination is fed directly to your senses from the brain. It would not be out of focus.'

However, as if to contradict that demonstration of impressive logic and to further illustrate Roy's critical appreciation of his encounter, he notes that when the figure vanished at its quite amazing speed there was no sound: 'Yet, surely, if it was a material object, the air rushing in to fill the vacuum at that spot would have made a sound. Why was there none?'

There we have the real problem that confronts us. What sort of scientific phenomenon can be physical and subjective, consistent yet individual, real and unreal — all at the same time?

7.

Monster Reality

Asked whether the position of the electron remains the same, we must say 'no'. If we ask whether the electron's position changes with time, we must say 'no'. If we ask whether the electron is at rest, we must say 'no'. If we ask whether it is in motion, we must say 'no'.

Professor J.R. Oppenheimer, nuclear physicist and 'father' of the atomic bomb

We have a major problem — a paradox — in our search to find what lies behind these monster stories. But we can comfort ourselves in the knowledge that we are not alone. Psychology faces the same kind of dilemma when it seeks to comprehend the nature of mind. And, as the quotation from J.R. Oppenheimer demonstrates, twentieth-century physics is struggling too.

I believe it is not only comforting to find these direct comparisons, but it is fundamentally important. What I am now about to do is try to put psychology, physics and monster apparitions together into the same cooking pot and see how the resultant stew might taste.

Let us start with the recognition that there seems to be three key elements in the experiencing of *monster reality*. These are the place where the event occurs, the person who is at the root of the experience and the state of consciousness within which they appear to be immersed.

Our task now is to analyse each of these components in turn

and find out what current scientific thinking has to say about them all. Then we can discover whether the facts just uncovered on our monster safari are in any way explicable by these processes.

I predict that a few surprises will be waiting.

We have already noticed some patterns in the location where monster events take place. Leaving aside the predominance of 'bedroom visitors', which seem best related to states of consciousness, we frequently found references to hills, mining areas, quarries, lakes and marshes. Quartz-bearing rock (and sandstones) also cropped up on a couple of occasions.

About twenty years ago researchers in France began to speculate about the number of UFO sightings that appeared along major fault lines in the earth, i.e. breaks in the rock below the surface which are constantly under strain. These sections gradually move relative to one another and most often the strain is relieved over a lengthy time period or held in check by other forces. In certain parts of the world where the strain is too great it can erupt in a very dramatic way, effectively 'breaking' with a 'snap' that results in what we call devastating earth tremors or earthquakes.

Geologists have known for years that prior to some major earthquakes, and during their occurrence, there have been reports of glows in the local sky not unlike the aurora found in polar latitudes.[109] Whilst research into the causes of these effects has been limited, it is now accepted that some form of ionization is being generated in the atmosphere by the stress and strain of the rocks that are under pressure. This electrical effect 'glows', rather like the 'arcs' of light in the vicinity of electricity transformers or power sources, such as masts and towers.

The first researcher to try to link this concept with paranormal phenomena was Dr Michael Persinger, a Canadian specialist in electromagnetic effects on the brain. With a colleague he set about comparing a large number of reports of 'strange phenomena' within the geographical and geological environment and claimed to find clear statistical correlations. From this he began to devise an extensive theory.[110]

As Persinger developed his work he soon reached a hypothesis something like the following.

In areas where there are active fault lines below the surface (and that is a high percentage of any land mass) stress and strain could find release into the atmosphere via physical processes. This would be especially notable in zones without frequent earth tremors, where a kind of 'leakage' might reduce strain and dilute the ultimate quake when it was inevitable.

The presence of hills in the fault areas would enhance the likelihood of discharge which would result from strain on rocks rich in quartz. In such rock the pressure would allow the quartz crystals to vibrate and generate a small electric charge by a process known as the *piezo-electric* effect. The same process is used artifically in certain types of lighter, generating power by pressuring a tiny quartz crystal. On the grand scale of a large fault and local hill system the result would be a far more substantial discharge, which could ionize the atmosphere and create glowing masses.

Because of the properties of electrical discharge, the masses would be more probable in certain locations, such as around towers or electricity pylons on the hills. Water would increase the resistivity of surface rocks and lead to greater luminous displays near any lakes within fault zones. Water would also change the likely ionization colour from bluish-white to red, because of the breakdown of hydrogen gases.

Quite probably some 'trigger' mechanism would initiate the leakage — something as simple as the passage of a heavy air pressure system (i.e. a change in the weather), or the gravitational pull of the full moon, or even artificial stimulation such as quarrying, mining or building work. As the strain 'leaked' through what could be several glowing discharges the rocks might finally release all the pressure at once in a small earth tremor. This would terminate a spate of luminous discharges, thus providing an initial 'wave' of reports in a short spell, which would either peter out as the strain subsided, or cease rapidly in conjunction with the tremor.

Persinger called such an 'electric column' a *transient*. He believed they would be of short duration (hence the name), but could move along the fault for up to several minutes, giving rise to what most people nowadays would perceive as UFOs, but in earlier times might have been interpreted according to local culture or legend.

However, he went further, incorporating his own field of research, by speculating that the physical effects associated with the electric field (e.g. interference on radio sets, car engines and possible 'electric tingles' or even burns to a witness who came too close) might cause the transient to appear intelligent. Also that very close exposure might lead to paralysis, affect the neurons in the brain leading to 'false smells' and other bodily disfunctions and provoke 'dreamy conditions, not unlike epileptic auras . . . (which) may include sensations as if the body was floating, or as if the self was leaving the body, alterations in time sequences, or sensations of meaningfulness or cosmic significance'.[111]

Surprisingly few people within paranormal research saw the dramatic way in which this concept matches up with a great deal of the evidence being produced from the field.

Nor should it be limited to UFO encounters, because if one of Persinger's transients were seen in the vicinity of a lake, for example, then it might appear to be a monster. This is significant when we realize that Loch Ness (like many other lakes in northern latitudes) lies right across a major fault zone and owes its existence to this geology; and when we recall how many monster cases feature bad smells, oz factor sensations or glowing red 'eyes'.

Independently of this work, Professor Helmut Tributsch, a physical chemist in Germany, was taking a close look at reports of highly unusual behaviour of animals in the period immediately before earthquakes. In certain countries (e.g. China) they were regarded, even in the twentieth century, as more reliable 'alarms' than any yet invented by science.

His research began with an earthquake in northern Italy on 6 May 1976. From this he collected reliable reports of cats that ran off into hiding with their kittens, dogs making strange noises, etc., all just before a major tremor. He found that on average the animals' behaviour altered radically from about 21 hours prior to an earthquake. He concluded that they must be repsonding to some sort of geophysical process occurring in the area around the fault line. Somehow the animals were attuned to this, although humans did not seem to be as susceptible.

Tributsch began to search through the possible processes which the animals might be reacting to. He ruled out sound, because too many species with widely differing hearing ranges were involved. Eventually he settled on changes in the electro-magnetic fields around fault lines as the most probable cause. However, his problem was why similar effects did not happen prior to thunderstorms, which also dramatically change the local electric fields.

Eventually, the Tributsch detective work settled on electrical ionization. He believed that positive ions released from the rocks by the quake as it built up were absorbed by animals who lived on, or close to, the ground. These in turn altered the balance of certain chemicals in their brains, notably serotonin, a powerful behaviour-affecting hormone, resulting in their alarmed reactions.

However, Tributsch rejected the piezo-electric effect as the cause of this ionization, because he believed the conductivity of moisture in the rocks near the surface would prevent the ions leaking into the atmosphere. He argues that piezo-electricity is generated and this stays in the rocks, breaking down water and dissolved minerals, giving off gases and sulphurous odours. Then different electrical processes in the spaces between rocks discharge ions into the atmosphere. He suggests that sudden and unusual banks of mist or fog, created by these ion-rich gases (and possibly even glowing like radiation clouds), might emerge from the ground near fault zones. [112]

Whilst this chemist was only talking about cases where major earthquakes have occurred and had no apparent knowledge of Persinger's work, we can see that he has really extended and enhanced the concept of electric column transients. Assuming, as we surely can, that smaller-scale versions of this ion leakage might occur from fault lines that are active, but not prone to erupting in a major destructive tremor, then we would antici-pate that our monster cases should offer strange reactions amongst animals and the presence of unusual clouds, mists and fogs in the vicinity of the creature.

Both of those predictions are amply fulfilled by our case material.

Whilst these scientific investigations were occurring, Paul Devereux, a Welsh expert in earth mysteries and stone-circle sites, was testing his own belief that UFOs were related to fault lines. By studying cases in one county (Leicestershire) and correlating them with the faults in the region, he persuaded himself to expand the study to a larger area. Working with a group of people, including geologist Dr Paul McCartney, he published his thesis in book form in 1982.[113]

Devereux also proposed that there were geophysical processes occurring, very much as Persinger and Tributsch had concluded. He argued that they were widespread and commonplace, invented the term 'earthlight' to encompass them and speculated that certain stone-circle sites might have been built in an area where they have always manifested and which thus appeared to the ancients to possess special significance.

Devereux and his team found several areas of Britain where there were many fault lines, and coincident with this many reports of strange lights. He noted the mountains of south-west Dyfed in Wales in particular but also commented on a puzzling gap. He suggested that there should be a UFO hot spot in the Pennine hills on the Lancashire/Yorkshire/Derbyshire borders, but claimed not to have recognized one in his rather limited search through one group's UFO data.

As if on cue, shortly after his book appeared, I published my report on the historical pattern of intense UFO activity in this *precise* location, which I had noted from the field without any knowledge of Devereux and his work. I had incorporated Persinger's early research, because I had seen its significance. However, the way my book plugged the very gap that Paul Devereux had recognized from his studies, must I feel effectively prove that there is something in these correlations.[114]

Not all researchers have supported this concept thoroughly. Some reasonable criticisms have been levelled, notably by Canadian astronomy graduate, Chris Rutkowski, who points out that much of Persinger's original data came from barely investigated cases and was, therefore, very probably overstocked with misperceptions, such as aircraft, stars and the like. Surely these can have no correlation with fault lines?

A similar comment could apply to Devereux's work. And Rutkowski has not been happy at the continued failure to find an acceptable way in which the ionization can be generated. Devereux, and to some degree Persinger, have now forsaken the piezo-electric process, but have not yet found any adequate replacement.[115]

On the other hand, several important laboratory experiments have taken place attempting to reproduce on a small scale the types of rock placed under the strain conditions found in nature.

Dr Brian Brady of the US Bureau of Mines in Boulder, Colorado, first achieved this in 1981 when he used extreme slow motion film to show up the very short-lived and tiny glows that accompanied a piece of rock being crushed to breaking point. In 1983 Paul Devereux, Paul McCartney and others reproduced the effect in London, witnessing orange glows and 'on one occasion, a delicate, tiny blue light of exquisite inner complexity moving in a geometric flightpath around the granite core under pressure'.[116]

Continuing investigation by these teams has ruled out the idea that the glows are plasmas and found that no microwave radiation is emitted. But Persinger *et al.* still believe some radiation is associated. In 1988 he was even speculating that paranormal researchers were at greater than average risk from certain cancers or brain tumours because of overexposure to sites where these transients are common. He also reports that some people — those who are 'creative' and who have frequent experiences of paranormal phenomena — may be more likely to suffer the effects of close proximity to one of his ionizing columns, simply because of the areas in their brain that are most active and open to electrical stimulation.[117]

This finding once again matches our discoveries in the field about witnesses to monsters having a psychic track record.

In 1989 major research is going on around the world in 'window areas' where UFOs are widely seen:[118] in Hessdalen, a remote Scandinavian valley where multicoloured lights appear with considerable regularity; in the USA, where Greg Long has been studying centuries-old traditions of orange balls of light in and around the Indian reservations of Yakima in Washington State; and in Britain, where Project Pennine is compiling considerable evidence that light phenomena have manifested in this geologically appropriate area throughout history.[119]

Far too much of this research fits in with what we have seen reflected in the evidence. Clearly, we must accept that at certain locations around the earth, which are sometimes called 'win-

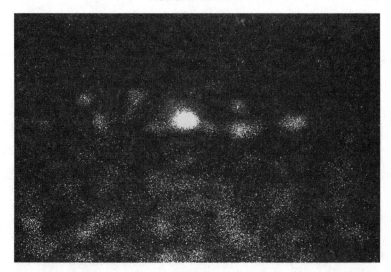

As the text explains, there are *window areas* in many parts of the world where it is speculated that geophysical processes can create glowing lights in the sky. Possibly these induce various types of *monster reality*. One of the most active locations during the eighties has been Hessdalen, a remote valley just south of the Arctic Circle in Norway. Scientific expeditions have provided some excellent photographic and instrumental evidence of these unexplained atmospheric glows, such as these bluish lights. Are these ionized gases which precipitate *mind monsters*? (*Project Hessdalen*).

dow areas', some geophysical process not yet fully understood is creating local ionization effects.

These transients, as Persinger calls them, need not always be visible. An electric field can be present and lead to tangible sensations and effects whilst having no actual form. Possibly at times particles of dust or vapour are attracted together like tiny magnets and may produce a gaseous/amoeba-like blob that has electric and radiative properties. At other times it could be the ionization itself, or Tributsch's ground-emitted gases which produce the luminous effect.

This goes by a variety of names, from Paul Devereux and his earthlights to what Hilary Evans terms BOLS (balls of lights). In this text I have been speaking of 'blobs' precipitating strange encounters. Quite probably these are all the same thing.

A mistake that many people are making is to connect these

blobs only with UFOs. Because we have approached the subject from a quite different angle and looked specifically at monster reports, we can see that there is no need to limit this work. The same features are occurring in reports of phantom cats, bigfoot, and assorted varieties of monsters and aliens.

Let us assume that these window areas *are* indeed generating blobs. What we now have to do is understand the process that is turning some blobs into UFOs and others into monsters. And how — if all that lies behind the stories are simple glowing lights — can consistent and apparently credible reports of differing creatures all come about? Even to the point of offering limited and yet intriguing photographic evidence?

The clues are already there. Both Persinger and Devereux have noted that around their transient/earthlight hot spots there is often noted a spate of poltergeist activity. Sudden, unexpected energies appear to move objects around a house, seemingly without physical cause and by the powers of the mind alone.

In conversations with Paul Devereux we have broached the subject of the mind interacting with his earthlights. He seems to feel the witness can sometimes not merely observe it, but on occasions can *manipulate* or *mould* it like putty. On the other hand Persinger says it is the blob that is affecting the brain and thus the mind's perception of what is there.

Which of them has the right explanation? Or, as we may now find, are both of them equally correct?

In order to try to answer this question we should move on to our second area of enquiry and explore what we know about the people to whom these various monster experiences occur.

We have seen quite a lot of evidence about the sort of people who have these monster experiences. I should stress that all that evidence strongly implies them to be, in the main, both sincere and stable personalities.

As I write a very interesting case has come to my notice from a puzzled and extremely lucid young woman who wants complete anonymity. She is a classic percipient of many of these things and comes from an impeccable family background. In addition she has qualifications in psychology and sociology and a university degree. As she herself explains: 'I know the symptoms of schizophrenia and similar disorders. I do not have them. These things sound incredible and I do not expect anybody to believe them. But everything that I tell you is true and without exaggeration.'

That she is being honest is supported by every study so far carried out into such people by psychologists and psychiatrists. Wherever else we must look for the answer, it appears not to be the field of mental illness.

Yet this clashes jarringly with the sort of things that these witnesses report. Here are just three examples.

We have already met Paul Bennet from Yorkshire. His life history involves so many monster apparitions they became almost normal to him. Aged 11 he saw a 'robot' in a quarry-like area beside a reservoir. Aged 12 he met a tiny furry figure 'with a head like a squashed tomato'. Aged 13 he encountered an 'angel' named Sigma in his bedroom. And so it goes on with countless sightings of blobs (UFOs), strange dreams, premonitions, etc. One of the most interesting to me was when Paul reported a UFO over an Ilkley Moor stone circle and later received a mild electric shock when touching the millstone rock there. Nigel Watson concluded from all of this that Paul Bennet, who is an avid reader and philosopher, had grown up with a different concept of what is real and what is unreal and so accepted experiences that others would dismiss. At the time I commented: 'Can Paul Bennet be a case of an extraordinary person in an extraordinary location resulting in a plethora of extraordinary events?'[120]

BUFORA investigator Ken Phillips has recently completed his research into a young woman from a north London council estate. Her lifestyle is fascinating. She has limited education, stays indoors through a phobia much of the time, but is highly artistic, writes songs and poetry, produces beautiful needlework and colourful paintings. At age 13 a 'blue light' entered her bedroom and a tall male figure 'materialized' from it. After that regular visits took place and she had long telepathic conversations about the meaning of life. She learnt of her origins in Arcturus, was given alien poetry (which all rhymes in English — so surely emerges from her subconscious rather than outer space) and has now met Ishtar, an alien with a white face, triangular features and coal-black cat-like eyes.

As if to show this is not unique, Ken and colleague Steve Chetwynd also followed up the case of Jean, a lady from

Berkshire, who first wrote lengthy letters to me. Her experiences began at age 12, but fully developed when in 1961 she had changed her baby's nappy in the middle of the night and suddenly 'felt weird'. Two beings then walked through the wall and 'solidified' in a shimmering haze. They wore emblems with a triangle on and the word 'Ishtal Maxim'. They told her (by telepathy) that they came from the Andromeda galaxy (as did she). Visionary abductions followed where she visited their 'ship' and later lovely gardens on their 'planet'. Then she was given projected images of all that was wrong with the earth and her 'mission' to help put things right. Jean has a very interesting background: she has a highly religious mother, her father is a professional entertainer and she has a university degree. Her track record of psychic experiences throughout life (dreams, premonitions, seeing ghosts, etc.) is extensive. She is an excellent artist and the psychiatrist who studied her case with BUFORA insists that she displays no evidence of any psychosis.

I could list case after case like this, but it must already be clear that we are dealing with people who grow up differently. Throughout their lives they have strange experiences, incorporate them into their view of the world and actively encourage, rather than discourage, their occurrence. They are also nearly always exceptionally visually creative in some form. The experiences tend to blossom into full-scale contacts from mid-childhood onwards.

Christopher Kenworthy, who has studied dreams and childhood development, showed me his unpublished research which notes that in this same period of early school years, what is called REM sleep decreases markedly. Psychologists believe that this sleep (in which dreaming occurs) is the time when new learning is integrated into the subconscious. The child uses this process to draw boundaries between reality and imagination, objective and subjective truths. The loss of REM sleep can produce difficulties for the child in making distinctions and, Kenworthy suggests, some people may evolve with a different form of consciousness where they take far more note of imagery than the rest of us do. We react against it, often as a result of being told *not* to daydream or to forget something because 'it's just your imagination'. Those without such pressures at this crucial early age may become young adults with highly developed visual perception and creativity. They would be naturally more open to phenomena which we have been indoctrinated against by society and culture.[121]

I should add that by calling these experiences 'imaginative' or 'subjective', and noting that most of us reject them from our lives during childhood, does not mean they are worthless or unreal. We adopt these words merely out of prejudice. It could be that these creatively visual people are not gullible and hyper-imaginative, but open and receptive. We might be the victims of self-deception, by raising the drawbridge and repelling all boarders from the psychic world on an incorrect premise that they are irrelevant or unreal.

Who loses most — the person who sees these things and struggles to understand their reality level, or the blind man who can neither see nor understand and must resort to assuming they do not exist?

More and more psychologists, sociologists and folklore re-searchers are treating these phenomena not as mere illusions but as alternative potential realities.

Carl Jung, the world famous psychiatrist, knew this. Almost the last subject he studied before his death in 1961 was UFOs. He wrote a perceptive book about witnesses to such experi-ences (thus perceiving years ahead of others what the correct approach must be).[122] However, because he used the words 'a modern myth' in the title most people assumed he was dismiss-ing these visions from any reality. In fact he accepted them as a space-age update to an age-old problem and very clearly realized there was some physical substance. The UFO group NICAP even claim he wrote a letter to them just before his death admitting that he considered UFOs to be alien craft, although I suspect if he were still alive Jung would be very much involved in the sort of debate this book is all about.[123]

Nor is Jung's position isolated. Thomas Bullard is a doctor of folklore from Indiana who has spent the last few years im-mersed in this field and offered some perceptive and extremely detailed research. He is well aware that down through the ages there have been 'shamans' (or magic men, or psychics — choose your term) who have played the same role within each tribe or society. They are exactly the sort of people we now see repre-sented in our witness sample and who have acted as interfaces between the objective world and the subjective universe. It is through them that our monsters have been kept alive.

Yet Bullard reminds us that there is 'a more down-to-earth side as well . . . These aspects lend the solidity of physical reality to the phenomenon.' And, as he reminds us, 'folklorists have never resolved this mystery of the likenesses'.

To explain the way the stories *seem* like visions, yet share remarkable patterns around the world, science faces three options (just as do we in this study). First, societies may somehow learn the correct form of their visions just as they learn behavioural responses. Or, second, there could be something innate within the mind of a species — at a deep level where ideas converge. And, third, of course, it could be that these experiences represent a form of reality which only the creatively visual people are able to perceive.

Any one of these answers would resolve the problem, but it would be wrong to say that by assigning these phenomena to the province of creatively visual or imaginative witnesses we are necessarily affording them no more substance than hopes, wishes and dreams.[124]

Alawn Tickhill from Kent wrote to me commenting on this. He actually claims to be a sort of modern medicine man. His headed stationery lists his job profile as 'shamanic medicine ways of personal power and vision, shamanic craftwork, counselling and tuition'.

He believes that the witnesses to monster reality are having: 'non-deliberate shamanic experiences . . . (they) accord very much with the types of experiences which shamans deliberately seek, and therefore have little or no conceptual framework in which to fit them'. The UFO experience, or the presence of a lake-monster tradition, or a spate of big-cat sightings offer this framework and thus introduce logic and ordering into what are otherwise accidental visionary encounters.

As if to make my point, Alawn describes himself as a typical shaman: 'I have a high IQ — 156 on the Cattel scale — am an artist, good image maker, much of a loner, have a history of psychic-type experiences, etc.'

Of course, psychologists struggle just the same as the rest of us in trying to evaluate the nature of such visionary experiences. They invent names, like my oz factor, to describe states of consciousness. But this really does little to explain what brings them about in the first place.

If a person enters what the psychologists call a 'fugue' state and wanders off for hours or days acting as if he were another individual, is that because his fantasy life has taken over, or because he has become 'possessed' by a spirit? When a person starts to hear messages in his or her mind and assumes them to come from a dead person or a spaceman and sets himself (or more usually herself) up as a medium, clairvoyant or abductee, is that because the voices come from his or her own fantasizing mind and he/she is ignorant of this fact, or because he/she is truly receiving some sort of communication that other people cannot perceive? These questions have no adequate answers, and will not have any whilst science continues to treat the paranormal as if it were an academic AIDS carrier. [125]

However, all is not completely lost. There is some very exciting work going on in psychology at the moment. It really began in 1983 when two Americans published a paper on their testing of a group of 52 highly intelligent people (several of who possessed degrees or even doctorates).

Theodore Barber and Sheryl Wilson were interested in what made a person a good hypnotic subject, so they compiled extensive psychological profiles of 27 women who were very easily put under the influence and 25 who were almost impossible to hypnotize. What they found was that almost all the good subjects 'had a profound fantasy life, their fantasies were often "as real as real" [and they have] vivid memories of their life experiences.'

They labelled these people 'fantasy-prone personalities' (fpps) and suggested that about 4 per cent of the population might be so designated (i.e. as many as 1 in 25 people).

Among the things that Barber and Wilson found about the fpps was that most had grown up believing in elemental beings such as fairies and many still thought they had seen them: 58 per cent had invented fantasy playmates as children (as opposed to just 8 per cent in the control sample of poor hypnotic subjects). Almost all of them confused their fantasies with reality from time to time, since they were so vivid, and likened the experiences to being 'inside' a 3-D movie in which they were taking part without knowing the script.

Many reported that when in idling states of consciousness (e.g. driving alone) they had had to pull up and stop because they saw figures ahead (e.g. a child). The figures were not there in reality. Some considered these figures to be ghosts wandering about and which they just had the ability to see with regularity.

Among fpps 95 per cent recalled in considerable detail events in their lives before the age of three and a third could recall scenes from just the first few months of life. This is a factor I have found with a number of victims of monster reality, not because I knew the question was relevant but because the witnesses themselves had realized it was unusual enough to mention. I am confident in predicting that if paranormal researchers ask this question in future interviews we will find that an overwhelming majority of percipients of monster reality share such early life recall.

I should add that the Barber and Wilson control sample demonstrated just a 12 per cent recall of this type of memory and from asking members of my immediate family that does not seem to be an underestimate. So the extreme levels of recall of fpps are clearly unusual and significant.

As we might predict, 92 per cent of fpps had lengthy track records of psychic experiences, far in excess of the occasional strange thing that might happen in an average person's life. Common amongst experiences reported were empathy with loved ones, telepathic messages, premonitions, out-of-body experiences, vivid apparitions, and near death visions of a life beyond. (These are listed in descending order of the extent to which they were reported in the study, but even the near death visions were many times more common than with the control sample — and generally this psychic bias was six to ten times more commonplace with the fpps than with the non fpps.)[126]

Two years after this work was published, Susan Myers and Harvey Austrin at St Louis University extended it to 200 individuals, including males and females, and found exactly the same pattern. They did note that women were more likely fpps than men and estimated about 3 per cent of the population could be labelled fpp based on their results. But these were just the extreme fpps. Their work offers a useful breakdown which shows that everyone has some rating on a kind of fpp league table.

If we call true fpps those who score over 80 per cent on the imagery testing, then this is where the 3 in a 100 result comes from. Conversely only 7 out of 100 score less than 25 per cent and so are very poor imagers. The majority of the population comes somewhere in between, although there are more people who scored under 50 per cent than scored above it. So good fantasizers or creeative visualizers are rare. Only 1 in 20 people rated above 75 per cent on the imagery scale.[127]

More work has followed. In 1986 and 1987 Steven Lynn of the Ohio State University and Judith Rhue of the University of Toledo reported on discoveries that fpps are often highly creative and seem to have suffered loneliness or severe punishment as a child. They had developed their imaging talent at that crucial age as either a way to combat being on their own or as a distraction from the pains and sufferings they were enduring.[128]

In 1988 this research was picked up by Keith Basterfield, the researcher into paranormal experiences mentioned earlier. He had already developed the idea that witnesses were frequently having hallucinatory experiences and this work fitted perfectly with his concept.[129]

Combining talents with Robert Bartholomew, a sociologist at South Australia's Flinders University, Basterfield and Bartholomew set about studying biographical records of 154 individuals who had claimed contact with alien creatures. They wanted to see if there were any indications that such people might match the fpp characteristics isolated by this earlier research.

Indeed there was clear evidence of this, although the main problem is that most investigators of monster reality (be they cryptozoologists, UFOlogists or psychic researchers) pay very little heed to the witness. They are working on the belief that the events witnessed are real and questions about creativity, visualization, psychic track records and family background are at best irrelevant and at worst intrusive and derisory of the percipient and his sanity.[130]

If we are to progress with our understanding of monster reality, that attitude simply has to be overcome and I hope that books such as this one may help some investigators understand why it is essential that the human component in all these cases cannot be overlooked.

In 1988 Bartholomew and Basterfield also published a very important article in the UFO literature attempting to explain cases of alleged abduction. I should stress that this theory is equally relevant to all other aspects of monster reality. The UFO abduction is nothing but the latest fashion — certainly in the view of Bartholomew, Basterfield and myself.[131]

They look at the three main theories in current vogue to explain abductions. These are most distinctly expressed by Budd Hopkins, who contends that real aliens are kidnapping people in actual physical reality,[132] parapsychologist D. Scott Rogo, who argues that the abduction is a psychic projection or 'objectified dream' acting out personality conflicts and created via the mind of a psychic witness,[133] and my own concept of an alien civilization that is only able to communicate through the mind of creatively visual people and which extracts data and causes visionary experiences almost as a side-effect of this long range probe.[134]

The two Australians found problems with each theory and proposed that the best solution is that fpps are simply having vivid fantasies of contact with aliens which are so realistic that they cannot distinguish them from reality. The fantasies occur, not through any psychosis or trauma, but purely because the person has evolved as a continuous fantasizer.

All three of the theorists (Hopkins, Rogo and myself) responded to this proposal.[135] Predictably, Budd Hopkins totally rejected the idea and argued that the psychiatrists he has worked with reject it also; although he has published no evidence to support this and I know of no life-profile testing of the creativity of his witnesses.

Scott Rogo welcomed the fpp idea as an area for research, but was doubtful of its validity. He believes that amongst its problems are Bartholomew and Basterfield's efforts to explain physical scarring which Hopkins has found (and photographed) on the bodies of several abductees. Hopkins contends these are the results of surgical operations by aliens. Rogo appears to feel some physical intelligence must have caused them. The fpp hypothesis only copes by suggesting that the witnesses were themselves responsible through the power of their mind and psychosomatically injured their own bodies because they believed in the fantasy so much.

In my view, these scars are not of proven significance. I have scars on my legs and I don't know where they came from. Was I secretly abducted? I suspect it is all too easy to have a strange experience, find a previously unnoticed physical mark and unconsciously connect the one with the other. And until I see evidence demonstrating that abductees have more — and quite unique — scars than a cross-section of the population who have not been abducted, it is not wise to accept this as proof of alien surgery.

On the other hand there are significant signs of physical reality within these cases for me to be very reluctant to accept a purely psychological solution. How would we explain Doc Shiels' flat 2-D photograph of Nessie — say that he lied? How would we account for the recurrent cases where very obvious forms of emitted radiation seem to be involved — put them down to coincidence? And how do we explain that all over the world the same monsters are being seen and the same stereo-typed aliens encountered? Surely fpps with gifted imaginations would have a wide range of fantasies, not hackneyed and repetitive examples such as those that we observe.

In a series of communications with me while I was writing this book Keith Basterfield explained that, although he believes fpps are responsible, he is uncommitted as to where the imagery comes from. It may be our own subconscious or an alien intelligence, and he would be equally happy with either given sufficient evidence. He also tells me that American psychologist Kenneth Ring, a leading expert in cases of near-death visions, is currently studying 60 such witnesses, alongside 60 UFO close-encounter victims and a control group of ordinary people. His testing for fpp traits will be fascinating.

Basterfield and Bartholomew's idea is that any physical effects associated with these experiences may be the product of psychosomatic factors. (Psychosomatic literally means 'mind' over 'body' and there is impressive support from scientific records that this can happen.)[136]

For example, experiments using nothing but willpower have shown that a surprisingly high percentage of women can enlarge breast tissue by a strong belief in its possibility. Doctors are also used to prescribing pills known as placebos. They contain harmless and ineffective (therefore *cheap!*) ingredients, but patients are not aware of the useless nature of their medication. Their conviction that by taking the tablets they can get better is often completely effective. Cancer specialists are equally aware that the desire to fight the disease can be as important as any medication that can be given.

On a more physiological level we have a number of well-attested cases of what are often called 'hysterics', patients who enter such a frenzied state of emotional anxiety that physical marks can be produced on their body. For instance, one patient who was repeatedly whipped as a child had a long-standing trauma resulting from that barbarity. Years later, when in a state of heightened tension, red weals similar to whiplashes appeared spontaneously on the victim's body.

Psychologist Dr Stan Gooch even reports one case where a man, through force of circumstance (alone in the jungle with a young baby to protect) produced milk and successfully breast-fed the child.[137]

Any stage hypnotist can further demonstrate that it is possible to trick a person into believing a chair is hot and he or she will 'feel' that heat. In certain extreme cases burn marks have been known to appear after this sensation which had no actual reality outside of the mind.

Can the mind cause physical effects? In the autumn of 1978 a man in the West Midlands had a vivid dream of a UFO. During the same night his neighbour claimed (without knowledge of this 'dream') to have seen a strange glow above the garden. In the morning the man awoke to find congealed blood on his wrist which appeared to spell the leters 'UFO' (UFOIN/BUFORA).

All of which goes to show that it is certainly possible for a limited number of people (and fpps would be excellent candidates) to become so absorbed in mental reality that the mind has an influence over physical bodily processes, thus creating commensurate effects.

One of Wilson and Barber's fpp patients produced a wart on her skin merely because she *thought* (incorrectly) that she had been in contact with something that should have produced the disfigurement. Given that, then it is surely not impossible that some of the witnesses to monster reality might induce physiological effects through their deep involvement with the experience.

The most important finding of this research is the superiority of mind over matter. All the evidence points to our consciousness having the ultimate role in controlling what occurs or what manifests as reality.

I have adopted an analogy which sees the brain as a static water wheel in a smooth pond. To all intents and purposes it is a lump of dead wood. But if the water is tilted just a fraction, so that it flows under the influence of an invisible force we call gravity, suddenly the wheel turns and if we connect it to a transformer, mechanical energy is switched into electromagnetic energy and electricity is produced. The wheel is like the brain and the resultant energy the effects produced by the brain, but all the brain is doing is allowing one form of energy to change into another more tangible, visible form. The energy itself is a product of that invisible gravity field introduced into the system. Similarly, consciousness appears to 'drive the wheel' and be very much more fundamental than the brain.

So does the electrical energy associated with monster cases emerge as a product of our mind? Or is it there all the time, via Persinger's transients, simply being *used* and *transformed*?

Paranormal researchers are fascinated by what is called PK (psychokinesis) — the apparent ability some people claim to move objects by thought. Very rarely is this working in a conscious way (e.g. Uri Geller's supposed talent for bending spoons at will). Much more often it occurs when a person is in an altered state of consciousness and some emotional urge seems to get changed into physical energy.

One of the most fruitful areas of research is into the surprising number of people who have major problems working electronic equipment such as computers. It seems that some folk just scramble the electrical signals. It is as if their brains 'leak' energy and make life very difficult, with visual display screens going haywire, telephones crackling with static and electrical appliances burning out far too often.

In our study of cases we have seen this happen and it turns up quite frequently amongst witnesses. Remember the Cheshire design engineer, Roy Smith, who met a monster in his bedroom and suffered many electrical problems and mysterious (if ultimately meaningless) messages on his computer screen? He is by no means unique.

We likened the effects then to those of a poltergeist attack and in many cases witnesses to monster reality also suffer poltergeist outbreaks around their home. The normal interpretation of these is that some emotionally disturbed ghost or spectre (poltergeist literally means 'noisy spirit') has taken possession of the building. More refined parapsychological theories consider that a person with an excess of emotional energy (often someone going through puberty) can let off steam in some psychic fashion.

However, let us look briefly at a typical poltergeist case investigated by Dr Michele Clare of the Sheffield Society for Psychical Research. She is one of the few researchers who is aware of the links with UFO and other monster cases.

The events focus on a family in a typical (and not very old) house in South Yorkshire. The main percipient, named as just Mrs B, was in her late thirties at the time of the events (1980). Described as having a 'nervous personality and suffering from bad headaches' she is also prone to 'get very angry sometimes'. She was twice divorced; her second husband, just before the outbreak, was violent and ended up in a psychiatric hospital after causing Mrs B serious injuries. He was diagnosed schizophrenic.

Five children lived with Mrs B (ages ranging from just a toddler to a teenager) and two other adult relatives shared the building also. Although Mrs B has had strange experiences since childhood (implying she is the chief focus) the poltergeist only struck soon after they moved into the house in 1979.

The reported incidents are typical of such outbreaks. Mysterious sounds like rocks or pebbles scattering, noises of crunching glass and bangs and creaks. An odour described as 'like stink bombs' also filled the house — the hydrogen sulphide smell we have become familiar with from monster cases all over the world. The family dog also occasionally reacted oddly and avoided parts of the house.

Visually, there were vague shadowy forms drifting about the rooms and electrical problems, such as 'interference on the television set, record players and cookers turning themselves on' and various (often heavy) objects moving, apparently without the help of human hands. A cup of coffee, for instance, shot across the room and clobbered Mrs B.

Most interesting were the small pools of water that turned up on the floor as if out of nowhere. This is another regularly consistent feature of poltergeist cases, but in this instance Mrs B says she once saw the pool forming in mid air. It was like a mini rain cloud dripping the water.

Almost all of these features fit perfectly with the idea of transients: the rock noises, gases emitted, electrical effects, vaporous forms and — most intriguingly — the puddles forming in mid air. Are these condensations of the emitted gases, heated up by the sudden temperature rise as they enter the environment of the house and turning from vapour into liquid form during the process?

This and other poltergeist attacks might be due to the presence of a suitable witness (such as Mrs B) in a location with a regularly active transient. The proposal can only be enhanced when we realize that the area in question has many mines and fault lines and hear the reason Dr Clare took this case so seriously. It was not reported publicly, but around the same time a second poltergeist outbreak with closely similar features occurred in a house on the same road and just a few hundred yards away. It appears that the two families had no connection and neither knew about the other strange reports.

The odds against that happening by chance are considerable. The best solution would seem to be that there was something special about the small area where the outbreaks occurred.

Modern psychologists and brain specialists have at their disposal marvellous equipment which science has developed. We can now, for example, take pictures of a living brain and with computers see which parts are active at any particular time. This has given us vast amounts of new evidence about the interrelationship between the mind and the brain.

There are two main parts to the brain, each of which is like masses of crinkle foil all screwed up together. This allows huge surface areas of cortex tissue to be enclosed within a much smaller space.

The cerebrum is the domed part at the top, normally thought of by most laypeople *as* the brain. It has two 'hemispheres', with the right hemisphere looking after the functions of the left side of the body and vice versa.

Yet underneath this, and to the back, is another much smaller area, which is about the same shape and not much larger than a walnut. This is called the cerebellum. Although it appears far less important, its cortex tissue is highly convoluted. Despite its apparent size of only one-tenth that of the cerebrum, it actually has three-quarters of the surface area.

We are learning a great deal about the differing roles of the cerebrum and cerebellum and the two hemispheres of each. For example, a tricky medical procedure known as 'split brain surgery' is sometimes now used by expert physicians as a means to curb extreme cases of epilepsy. Effectively the links between the two cerebral hemispheres are cut. This does not stop either one working, but rather like cutting Australia off from the rest of the world, it means there is limited communication between the two sides.

This is useful in terms of epilepsy, because it restricts the chain reaction of firing cells to a small part of the brain and prevents total surrender to the electrical maelstrom.

Some people are born with just a fraction of the cerebral cortex of other humans, yet all the functions of the cerebrum are incorporated into what little remains and several of these patients have grown to become completely normal individuals with high IQs and university degrees. Others have large sections of brain removed and they do not become vegetables. It appears that functions are spread around the whole brain in such a way that, although one region has prime control over something, part of that control is invested almost everywhere else as well.

On the other hand, the severing of links between the hemispheres has some interesting side-effects. For instance, if the right eye is covered and a nude picture is shown to a split-brain patient, the information comes in via the left eye and so only reaches the right cerebral hemisphere. The patient usually cannot name what he is seeing, but may blush. So there is subconscious awareness of the picture content (and indeed he could visually select the appropriate one from a pile of examples) but the verbal expression of the name associated with the image is lost.

Most scientists assume this has been lost in the surgery. Of course, all that may actually have been lost is the control over body functions allowing expression. There are reasons to believe that all abilities remain intact at a subconscious level.[138]

From fascinating research such as this we are uncovering the complex responsibilities of the brain. Oversimplifying things we can say that the cerebrum is responsible for logical, rational, constructive and conscious principles, whereas the cerebellum has far more to do with intuitive, instinctive, emotional and unconscious processes. The former operates through facts, figures, patterns of order and sensory input and objectivity that determines time and space, thus telling of the 'real' world. The latter uses symbols, imagery and feelings that work in magical, coincidental and synchronistic ways, leading to poetry or fiction and telling of the 'dream/imaginary' world.

It may not be unconnected that the cerebrum is physically larger and sits on top of the cerebellum. The cerebral traits are what we normally ascribe to the male ethos ('feet on the ground' rationality) and the cerebellum has a lot more to do with the female spirit (creativity, emotion and 'woman's intuition'). An awareness of these truths has always affected society. This may be why we seem to think of the conscious mind as being *on top* of the unconscious mind, why we speak of dreams and images being *below the surface*, why we liken mythical places to abodes such as the *underworld* and possibly even why women have for centuries been suppressed by men and accepted that suppression.

This is important in the context of our present discussion when we try to decide what state of consciousness exists within a witness when he or she is immersed within monster reality.

Look at the clues: the Oz factor, which implies that the real world is where the events occur, but with a sudden intrusion of dreamy, subjective states; the loss of awareness of space and time; the way that symbology and images become important in the resultant cases; and the bizarre way coincidences synchronize together and provide a logically inexplicable interplay between 'hard fact', 'imagined fact' and 'fictional creations'.

We tend to think in simple terms, assuming something is black or white, real or unreal, factual or imaginary. But science does not support that argument. Colours come in a spectrum and nothing is completely black or totally white, just myriads of subtle shades in between. Likewise the cerebrum and cerebellum do not exercise total control over one side of life. In every person there is a balance. Some may have a more active cerebrum (the sort of person we might call a realist); others have a very effective cerebellum (we might call them dreamers), yet all of us have elements of both.

I believe the same to be true of our states of consciousness and what we perceive as the reality we are currently living through.

At the two extremes are the 'real world' (of facts, conscious sensory input and the cerebrum), and the 'dream world' (of emotions, unconscious imagery and the cerebellum). Normally, when 'awake' we are close to the 'real world' end of the spectrum and when 'dreaming' we are close to the 'dream world' extremity. At other times we are somewhere inbetween, such as when hypnotized, idling on a boring car drive or falling asleep and waking up — which is why unusual visionary experiences can occur at these times.

The most amazing type of dream-world experience is what scientists call the lucid dream.[139] If you have experienced one of these (as I and many other people have) you will understand the use of terms like magical and unforgettable.

Basically, it is a dream during which you suddenly *realize* that you are dreaming. The conscious mind intrudes, then takes control and until you lose your grip and fall back into normal dreaming you have control over a fabulous Meccano set of images. You live *within* the dream, controlling the environment — I recall flying through a window and walking through a closed door because I knew I could make myself do anything in this reality. In this way the dream takes on an entirely new perception.

Since everything we know about the brain and mind suggests

that there is always an opposite, I would expect there to be an equivalent state of consciousness which we might call the waking lucid dream.

This would occur whilst the person was living in the 'real world' and instead of cerebral (conscious) control, the cerebellum with its unconscious emotions and images would seize the reins. Whilst the experience lasted our unconscious mind would have the ability to shape and mould the imagery at its disposal. This imagery, of course, would be the real world.

We could predict that the waking lucid dream would happen to people with strongly developed cerebellum (which appear to be mostly artistic and creative folk — or fpps) and that they would be in a real-world situation when something caused them to shift gears and let the cerebellum take command. They would become aware of this by conscious sensory input fading out and cerebral considerations (like time and space) taking a back seat. Then symbols, emotions and coincidences would start to tinker with the real world and the person would experience a vivid waking dream, from which he or she would eventually return to normal consciousness (i.e. 'wake up').

What would the percipient experience? I think you can see it would be the Oz factor, followed by an event that may well be 'impossible' in terms of normal waking reality, but which would almost certainly appear to have occurred *within* that normal waking reality, because that was the state of consciousness *before* and *after* the events took place.

This is what I believe happens when a witness enters *monster reality* and this is the explanation for many of the puzzles we have found in our series of cases.

Yet, whilst we may have understood that certain types of people can enter this altered state of consciousness, possibly when triggered to do so by a close encounter with a transient, and whilst we have seen that physical effects might result because of the powerful imagery and the understandable belief that the experience takes place in the real world, we still need to know how resultant monsters share features around the world or how a quasi-reality, in at least a photographable sense, seems to come about.

What exactly is reality? That is a question which has vexed philosphers, psychologists and physicists since we first began to probe the nature of life. The curious thing is that they are all now converging towards a consensus view, despite coming from very different backgrounds.

At the start of this century physicists still lived in a world that was ordered by Sir Isaac Newton. He developed most of the laws that allowed us to predict how things worked. This view — known as mechanism — said that the universe consisted of solid matter which could be broken down into ever smaller parts (from big bits, to grains, to molecules, to atoms and then to individual particles making up atoms). All one had to do was work out the sums and one could predict how everything would react in any circumstance.

The whole universe, from galaxies to human beings, came down to a series of equations which let reality be defined as akin to a Victorian factory with its various interlocking parts and moving gears.

However, between 1900 and the early 1920s that concept was completely overturned by atomic physicists such as Albert Einstein. By 1945 brilliant scientists such as J.R. Oppenheimer were making statements like the one at the head of this chapter. These sound like utter nonsense. Others spouted mysticism. One of the world's greatest physicists, Wolfgang Pauli, teamed up with psychologist/psychiatrist Carl Jung in an effort to understand the meaning of coincidence, thereby inventing the theory of synchronicity. Out of this Pauli was led to make comments such as: 'It would be the more satisfactory solution if mind and body could be interpreted as complementary aspects of the same reality.' His colleague, Sir Arthur Eddington, nodding sagely, added: 'The frank realization that physical science is concerned with a world of shadows is one of the most significant of recent advances.'

How did such a change come about? Essentially through probing into the atom and finding that this basic building block of the universe had many constituent parts (as everyone had expected) but that these parts in no way resembled the solid reality of the world that we experience. They were in fact a ghost reality. Clouds of probabilities lay behind everything, in which particles were created and died in fractions of seconds and had a form of existence that allowed *nothing* to be predicted with any certainty.

Newton would have said that if two atoms or bits of atoms were fired at one another they would behave like snooker balls, bouncing off in perfectly predictable ways and moving smoothly across the table. The reality of subatomic physics was more like two phantoms bumping into one another, passing straight through as if neither were there, winking out of existence and reappearing a fraction of a second later on the other side of the cosmos.

This sudden descent into statistics as the basis of reality is what bothers everyone about subatomic physics. In the 'real world' everything was logical and followed simple rules. Newton proved that and nobody has ever shown that he was wrong. Yet the particles that make up this real world just do not behave like that. The scientists say it is because at the macroscopic level — i.e. the world we see (where even a pinhead has billions of subatomic parts) — statistics even out and allow us to make the sort of predictions that are impossible at the microscopic level.

However, at the same time none of them knows how or why this operates. Or where the boundary lies between the microscopic and macroscopic world, i.e. the one we cannot predict and the one that we can. Indeed nobody knows if there is a boundary, because nobody has seen any clear sign of one.

We can get some idea of what is involved by tossing a coin. Toss it ten times and see what happens. There is no way I can tell you, or you can guess, the outcome. You might find that it lands on heads ten times, or tails ten times, or five times on each, or any result inbetween. But if you have the time and tenacity to toss the coin a thousand times, then I can predict with reasonable certainty that (give or take 10 or 20 either way) you will get about 500 head calls and 500 tails. Do the same thing a million times and the breakdown will be very close to 500,000 each.

Now toss the coin once more. The one million and first toss is in no way affected by what has gone before. If there are 499,999 heads and 500,001 tails the next toss is not more likely to be a head to 'even up the score'.

In just the same way we cannot predict individual subatomic reactions (except vaguely, i.e. it may be this or it may be that). But once we talk about millions of them happening all at once we can make very good approximations.

The consequence of this seems quite absurd. For example, the constituents of a pencil on a desk top are moving in random directions, under external influences such as gravity. There is no way we can say whether one of these constituents will move up or down, but we can predict with virtual certainty that the pencil itself will stay where it is and not suddenly leap up into the air. But it *could* do that. The fact that we have never seen a pencil jump up is due to the statistical probabilities of very large numbers under the influence of the known forces that operate. But it is *absolutely not* a certain outcome.

If something from outside could upset the statistics and introduce a new factor the pencil might be made to jump up. It would, in effect, behave as if it had become infected by a poltergeist or taken over by PK.

Similarly a gaseous vapour usually spreads out into a pretty amorphous shape (e.g. a blob) because its constituents are moving in random directions and the influence of operating forces are much less, ultimately causing the gas to dissipate as it spreads further and further apart. However, theoretically it is possible to change that situation.

For instance, free the gas inside a jar shaped like Mickey Mouse and it will spread out to adopt the shape of Mickey Mouse. This is due to the restraining forces of the walls of the jar, which are preventing further expansion. Suppose we now had a way of instantly dematerializing the jar — what would be left? For a brief moment there would be a gaseous cloud shaped like Mickey Mouse, which would quickly spread apart as it was now free of the restraining forces.

Perhaps you can see what I am aiming at. If there were a way that the mind could create or structure a field that already existed, and assuming the field was invisible to our normal senses (as most are, e.g. gravity, electricity, etc.) then subatomic physics positively supports the idea that we can use such a process to re-order physical matter.

A vapour is highly malleable for good physical reasons. We only need to look at clouds and see how these are endlessly shaped and reshaped by invisible forces like the wind, air pressure and gravity. If we had a gas cloud at a location where there was also a transient with its associated electromagnetic field, then theoretically there is no reason why we couldn't control that invisible field and 'bottle up' the cloud in any shape we chose.

As we have already seen, there is evidence that some minds can influence subatomic matter. If it is occasionally possible to exert a force that lets a cup of coffee suddenly take off and fly through the air, if it is even easier apparently to alter the patterns of an existent electrical field and interfere with TV or telephone reception, then it should not be impossible for the mind to impose itself on the fairly impressionable physical matter (e.g. gases) that we may find at transient sites. It may not be out of the question to suddenly shape the field so that it pulls together a gas cloud, or dust particles clinging together by electrostatic attraction. And if for some reason that field is fashioned into a monster, then a cloudy, amorphous, monstrous shape may suddenly loom up in front of the unsuspecting witness. Once out of the special state of consciousness (the waking lucid dream) then, of course, this temporary conjuring trick would cease and the field would collapse to its original state. As a result the physical matter shaped by it would vanish.

It is interesting that in a number of cases some 'residue' is found at sites of monster encounters. Sometimes these are sticky goos or ashes. Remember how at Mundrabilla in Australia black ash (later analysed as worn brake lining) was found after the 'black cloud UFO' disappeared? Is that because the ash had been caught up within the field and had created the UFO shape? Then, when the field (and so the UFO) collapsed, all that was left behind was the inert ash discarded at the spot.

Atomic physics has many close analogies to offer up. For instance, Werner Heisenberg, who proved that specific predictions could not be made at a microscopic level, called his result: 'a strange kind of physical reality just in the middle between possibility and reality'. Doesn't that sound rather like all we have learnt about monster reality?

One of the first clues to make physics question the old Newtonian view was the nature of light. In the nineteenth century physicists had shown it to be an electromagnetic field. Experiments that are still valid today prove this beyond any doubt. However, Einstein and others then showed that light came in a little packet called a 'quantum' (from which comes the term quantum physics, i.e. subatomic research). In fact Einstein won the Nobel Prize for *this* work, not his later relativity theories.

Again, it is possible to conduct experiments and prove conclusively that light is neat little quantum lumps like particles. But how can light be both particles and an electrical field at the same time? Isn't this just the question we face in the paranormal when we ponder how monsters can appear real and yet are clearly dependent upon subconscious and subjective forces?

Physics did not progress by proving light to be one thing and not the other. It accepted that it was basically an electromagnetic field which under certain circumstances took on the real guise of particles — a consequence of the way probability and quantum physics works.

I suspect the same lesson should be learnt within the paranormal. Monsters may just be a special case of a field taking on reality through a combination of circumstances.

Furthermore, we now know that the solid shapes of atoms are the product of nothing but clouds of whirling subatomic constituents at the microscopic level. Something — and science does not yet know what that something is — turns the confusing *mélange* into what we call solid reality.

Quantum physicists struggle to comprehend the origins of that 'something'. As early as 1927 a group of physicists got together in Brussels and came up with the Copenhagen Interpretation (so named because several of them hailed from that city). Essentially they opted out, saying that the crystallization of reality from these subatomic phantoms was just a statistical quirk that is not understood. This allowed them to get on with researching the results without worrying about the causes. Most physicists continue to use such reasoning because it ultimately works for them. They have not needed to understand the whys and wherefores in order to find what results in practice.

Einstein hated this idea of putting it all down to quirks of chance and statistics. He once made a famous remark to physicist Max Born: 'God does not play dice.' But he never found a better answer.

Since 1927 we have learnt a great deal, in particular that the outcome of the statistical juggling trick appears to be influenced by one important thing — the person who does the observing.

This was first demonstrated by Ernest Schroedinger, who designed an experiment (thankfully not carried out) in which a cat is sealed in a 'gas chamber'. A pellet of deadly gas will be triggered if — and only if — a radioactive subatomic particle decays in a certain way.

Statistically there is no way of predicting the outcome. Either the atom decays one way, the pellet is released, and the cat dies; or it decays the other way, the pellet remains sealed and the cat lives.

According to commonsense, the event takes place and if we open the box we will learn whether the cat is alive or dead. However, quantum mechanics shows that this is not the truth. Until we open the box the decay remains a probability wave with both possibilities just as likely. We only 'collapse the wave function', as physicists call it, when we open up the box. Then one or other option materializes out into a live or dead cat.

The idea of having a live/dead cat in limbo until we take a look and see which one it is seems outrageous. But this is what physics says must happen. Another physicist (Wigner) made it even more absurd by postulating a human being as the guinea-pig and asking him or her (if he or she survives the experiment!) what he or she felt like during the time he or she was in limbo.

To overcome even trickier, if more humane, experiments (some of which have now been carried out) the Copenhagen School just says that, obviously, something causes the wave function to collapse and the cat lives or dies. We just do not know what that missing factor is. Unfortunately, there is little evidence that supports the theory and some of the experiments now conducted seem to indicate that the subatomic world must have its own consciousness and make choices (even choices based on ESP!) if the missing factor is anything other than the human mind.

For that reason more and more scientists are now of the opinion that consciousness is indeed what collapses the wave function and that our mind, through the act of observing quantum events, turns them into what we perceive as the real world.

Those wanting to explore this incredible fantasy world of subatomic physics will find parallels galore, far more than I have space to discuss here. An excellent primer comes from Gary Zukov, who notes that as a consequence of all this: 'We begin to glimpse a conceptual framework in which each of us shares a paternity in the creation of physical reality.[140]

One of the latest theories to try to resolve the mess comes from American quantum physicist Jack Sarfatti who is proposing that it is not merely our minds which are necessary to explain the collapse of the wave function and how reality comes about; we also need the suspiciously mystical idea of all things being interconnected with one other.

He seems to be implying that at a quantum level the laws are those of synchronicity. Change something and it alters the universe a little, because each part is just a constituent of the greater whole. The atoms within our bodies are inextricably linked with us, just as we are inextricably linked with every other human being and all humans are part of the entire ecology of the planet, similarly the planet is linked with the universe, which may in turn be linked with something else (God?)

This hierarchical concept of the cosmos as a means of understanding modern physics is very exciting. It seems to offer us yet another link with monster reality.

We may have seen possible ways in which both physics and psychology are now suggesting that the mind might structure matter, and thus create monsters and even control what reality we perceive. Yet we still need to understand how our monster experiences can share so much in common.

They do not behave like individual fantasies projected from the depths of consciousness of a gifted imager. If that were so then surely we would be confronting reports of monsters of every conceivable shape and variety, like those which fill the episodes of *Star Trek*. Instead we have very limited and stereotyped apparitions that seem too consistent to be simple products of fantasy-prone imaginations.

However, if Sarfatti and others are correct then we have a connection between everyone at this quantum level where consciousness operates. That could make our problem a great deal easier to understand.

In 1981 Dr Rupert Sheldrake, a young British biologist, set the scientific world into frenzy with a book that the prestigious journal *Nature* described as one of the best candidates for public burning yet seen![141]

What crime had the researcher committed? He had challenged the long-held view that Darwinian evolution had all the answers. Indeed, a quiet revolution has been going on in biology and zoology ever since Crick and Watson discovered the DNA mechanism. This long strand of molecules contains the genetic code, i.e. the information that tells an animal what it is and how to grow and evolve throughout its life. But it has brought with it some very awkward questions. Every DNA molecule contains the same coded information to make one type of creature. Sheldrake was daring enough to ask how the body knew that a leg should grow here, and an arm there, and to grow muscle cells and not other organs, etc.

Furthermore, certain animals can be cut up and the parts will regrow into new animals. Elsewhere in the animal kingdom if a part of an animal is chopped off (e.g. a starfish arm), a new one will take its place.

The logical implication of all this is that as well as the DNA code there is a kind of invisible blueprint which tells the genetic information how to operate. This is not a chemical or atomic part of the structure, and it seems to be another of our invisible fields.

Sheldrake pointed out that if we want to build a house we need bricks (which he likened to atoms) and manpower (i.e. energy). But if that is all we have then the same bricks could build any number of houses. We also need a plan showing which bricks go where. DNA alone cannot do that with an animal, so he proposed that we also have a sort of life-shaping field which helps order the DNA. He called them morpho-genetic fields (or M fields).

M fields would help explain a number of other problems, for instance, how subjective information (emotional responses, perhaps even memories) is retained by a human being.

There is a real dilemma here. We may not realize it, but we are not the same person that we were a few years ago. And I mean that literally!

Every few years our bodies are completely renewed. We are shedding millions of atoms every day, through digestion, skin peeling off, hair falling out and so on. These are usually regrown, although as we get older some things do not get replaced as quickly or even at all. But none of us consists of any of the atoms that we were born with.

It only takes a moment's thought to recognize the blindingly obvious implication of this. Since our thoughts, memories and bodies appear to be the same as they were before, *something* must have made those new atoms follow the same pattern as the ones they are replacing. Again we seem forced towards the conclusion of an M field to form this missing template, advising nature and DNA how to 'build' an animal. Presumably dogs, cats, frogs and rats each have their own M field.

Sheldrake also questions the process by which instincts and learning are passed on. Some American butterflies, for instance, fly thousands of miles and mate in the exact same field as their predecessors. According to Darwin that is because the information to tell them how and where to fly was passed on through DNA by their parents. However, there are grounds for thinking this may not be the case.

A number of experiments were carried out in the USA which taught rats to learn how to escape from a pool of water without following the most logical course. That course would have brought an electric shock. As Darwin predicts, the first group took a certain number of tries to learn the painless escape route, but rats bred from them took less attempts. Eventually many less tries were needed by rats that came several generations later.

According to Darwin this was easy to explain: the rats learnt from previous generations, with information passed on from parent rat to child rat.

However, the same experiment was also carried out thousands of miles away with new rats which had no genetic link of any kind with those from the USA. Yet on the very first trial these took many less attempts than the first American rats. When the experiment was repeated, and more independent rats in another country needed even *less* moves, there was only one conclusion possible for Sheldrake, although other scientists rejected it with sheer horror, claiming this was just an attempt to make science out of magic.

Sheldrake argued that the second group of rats learnt quicker because of the success of their trained American predecessors. There was no direct link, but at the level of the M field they did not need one. Just as Sarfatti was speculating in his own field of quantum physics, Sheldrake proposed that habits, patterns of behaviour, evolutionary changes and information were shared between a species at some fundamental level.

His concept, which he called formative causation, said basically that if a group of animals in one species learn it is useful or essential to do something new, then any future animals will be able to do it as well. The learned behaviour of the successful rats has altered their individual M fields and these have in turned added up to change the collective M field of the entire species. Future rats pick up their behaviour by 'tuning in' to the collective field, which now incorporates the new behaviour.

Sheldrake explained the way in which this could work by the idea of resonance. In physics, if a musical instrument string is plucked at a certain frequency, then another string that is not connected in any way to the first one can issue the note as well. The first string produces an invisible energy wave and the other string has frequencies in common and so plays along in harmony.

Resonance is a common phenomenon. Everyone has experienced it. For instance, if we put a radio on and some metal object in the room starts to vibrate in synchronization with the music, it is probably because part of its structure is resonating with some of the frequences in the energy field issued by the music.

Sheldrake thus had the idea that an individual's M field could tune into the collective M field of the species and its pattern of behaviour would be determined by this. He called the procedure *morphic resonance* and assembled an impressive collection of evidence in support. He also made predictions and encouraged science to test his theory and prove it wrong.

It has to be said that every test carried out since publication seems to have vindicated the theory. New clues from natural history have constantly been brought to our attention.

Sheldrake published an updated version of his book which discusses some of the results and new leads and it is to their credit that not everyone was as churlish as *Nature*. The other leading science journal *New Scientist* sponsored a competition to find the best experiments and BBC television science programmes carried several others.[142]

Of course, Sheldrake was well aware that if it worked for rats it worked for humans too, as they too had a pattern of evolution, albeit on a less rapid time-scale. And here was where the supernatural consequences of the idea came into their own. These were certainly not lost on Sheldrake either, because he started receiving the leading journals in the paranormal field to look for new data and happily gave interviews discussing his work with sources such as *Fortean Times*.[143]

I have been impressed with the subtlety of some of the experiments. They include producing original nonsense rhymes in Japanese and seeing if English-speaking children can learn these any quicker than real nursery rhymes which millions of Japanese children have already learnt.[144]

In 1988, Sheldrake noted how sheep in Britain had learnt to walk across cattle grids. Humans can cross over because we are intelligent enough to know how to step on the metal bars without putting our feet in the holes. Sheep do it by going into a ball and rolling across! As soon as a few sheep picked up the trick, within months sheep all around Britain were doing it. Obviously, this was not communicated by any normal method, nor was there enough time for Darwinian evolution to pass on the habit through heredity. But morphic resonance works beautifully as an explanation.[145]

Sheldrake has this wonderful concept of a whole planet ecology possibly seething with M fields. There would be a hierarchical structure, just as Sarfatti suggested, with the more intelligent species contributing the most to the overall planetary consciousness.

Is this where we should seek the origins of our monsters? The idea of sharing our lives with ethereal cratures has been common throughout history. If Sheldrake is right then there have to be M fields associated with this imagery. Perhaps they are a consequence of all the main evolutionary groups.

Earlier on we speculated about dinosaur imagery resulting from vestigial impressions of the mammals who faced these creatures and required behaviour patterns to cope. If morphic resonance operates then we may still have access to some of these ancient templates.

Similarly, it is possible that bigfoot imagery comes from our pre-hominid ancestors. These would have been a source of great concern to many lifeforms on this planet and there could still be patterns left with which we would have some attunement by virtue of our hereditary connections.

I find it interesting that our monsters tend to be extreme forms of all the main species now on earth: dinosaurs — the ultimate peril for mammals; pterodactyls also — perhaps in the days of the first birds their major threat; sea monsters — a kind of nightmare behemoth for all current marine life; and the hairy man — the real nemesis of even larger mammals. Could these differing monster types be a kind of M field distillation of the main predators that stalked all lifeforms now conjoined within the lifefield of our planet?

Speculation this may be, but I can see how Sheldrake's theory fits into monster reality.

He says himself: 'In the early stages of a form's history, the morphogenetic field will be relatively ill-defined and significantly influenced by individual variants. But as time goes on, the cumulative influence of countless previous systems will confer an ever-increasing stability on the field; the more probable the average type becomes, the more likely that it will be repeated in the future.'[146]

We have some evidence for this from studies of the paranormal. Take the UFO. As a disc-like spaceship this is a modern motif. We have seen how in other decades UFOs were perceived in entirely different ways. When airships were observed in 1896 that was how the phenomenon manifested until the form changed. Was this because the M field temporarily stabilized into this concept of a UFO looking like an airship?

Then, come the spring of 1947, UFOs were erroneously reported by Kenneth Arnold as a formation of discs over an American mountain. If we look at the case records for those first years (e.g. 1947-52) we find a surprisingly large number of UFO formations — surprising, because in today's cases almost no formations occur. UFOs also then *became* discs.

We might account for this by suggesting that the M field 'UFO' was altered by the mass publicity given to the Arnold sighting. People then had their own experiences and these followed the pattern, with individual variations. Because so many people were seeing things, the M field gradually stabilized again and the formations became smoothed out of the pattern as it fixated on the classic disc shape. A great help in this stabilization process were the science-fiction movies of the early fifties which chose the single disc-like UFO as their theme and profoundly affected the UFO M field by reaching so many people.

Since the mid-fifties there have been smaller changes and new phases (e.g. the new abduction craze exploding over the past decade). But each shows the same internal mechanism, a gradual settling into a consistent theme as the individual variants get smoothed out — a theme so consistent it crosses cultural boundaries and so implies (perhaps falsely) that it is completely real.

The UFO perfectly matches Sheldrake's prediction of a developing M field. And I suspect that our other monster phenomena may display the same kind of natural history.

The idea of morphic resonance and M fields, coupled with everything else that we have discussed in this chapter, emerges directly from current scientific theory, plus the facts that we have uncovered in a search through monster cases.

Together they seem to suggest a successful explanation for monster reality.

Conclusions: Mind Monsters

The stuff of the world is mind stuff.

Sir Arthur Eddington, physicist

All over the world for countless centuries there have been tales of monsters. In the dim past on the threshold of humanity's awakening, these accounts were spread through the tribe by the storytellers and the shamans. It would even seem possible that we *perceived* them differently. In our infant years as a human race we were more in touch with our inner lives, better able to heed the cries of our unconscious or tune into the planetary field that scientists may now be merely rediscovering.

These effects remain, like echoes from a gong that was struck long ago. The energy is still reverberating, although fewer among us seem able to hear it than used to be the case.

And yet we *do* seem to need a 'fantasy' life. Living in the humdrum world of waking reality, forever drowning in sense impressions that are processed by the cerebral cortex, may be dangerous; these are threats as real — if not quite as tangible — as the sabre-toothed tiger or the mountain wolf. It may be that to keep us sane, to stop us seizing up with the goo of objectivity, we require frequent weekend breaks inside our head.

During those breaks we make contact again with the inner being, the world we meet in our dreams with its cerebellum imagery. This may provide us with the antidote to living in the 'real' world.

However, if we only faced a land awash with nightmares and

people hallucinating ancient terrors back into existence, this book would not have been necessary. The truth is more than that. The truth is fascinating.

Instead I have come to the conclusion that Persinger, Devereux and others are right — at least, partially right. In certain places there are haunted spots. We may use a pseudo-scientific term like 'window area' to disguise them, but it does not hide the magic or the reverence. If we were to detect and study them we would find lots of names that date back many centuries, with words such as 'devil' or 'demon' to hint at strange things which have always gone on in their vicinity. For we have long recognized their nature, long dwelt beneath their spell. All that has changed is our approach to these places. Now, instead of hailing them, we seek to dissect them beneath the microscope. We want to know what makes them tick. And we are beginning to do that.

We seem to have these windows everywhere, perhaps many in every country. Some are more active than others. But each has the right combination of geographical or geological factors which allow the processes to occur and conjure up their speciality. Although we do not yet comprehend all that happens, we are aware of the general trend. And this in turn can lead us into more research and hopes of demystifying the problem.

These window areas *appear* to be the result of natural processes, not supernatural laws. Here we find fields of energy (electrical, ionizing, magnetic, radiative) and these are somehow related to the place itself. Whilst most of us can pass right through them without being aware of the difference, there have always been people who are more sensitive. Perhaps long ago there were more of them, in an era when we had to be in tune with the environment, the seasons and the earth, because our very survival depended on it.

Today there still do seem to be people who can sense the opening of these windows. Maybe they are just those who are sensitive to electrical fields — the sort who prickle or tingle when a thunderstorm is gathering. Perhaps something in their brain responds to the energies that are garnered in these areas. Very probably we will be able to resolve these questions in the not too distant future.

However, whilst there are millions who might 'sense' the window, there seem far fewer who react to it. These, I propose, are the ones with well developed cerebellum, the creative and artistic who are excellent as visual imagers. Perhaps psychologists are studying them under the term 'fantasy-prone personality', mistakenly assuming that these people are just 'imagining' these experiences.

We have no proper justification in saying that fpps experience the world any less correctly than we do. In fact, as subatomic physics appears to imply, there are grounds for the opinion that it is *we* who are blinkered, and not they.

Reality is a collective opinion forged by mutual consent. If we do re-order the universe at a microscopic and statistical level then things are as they seem *only* because we choose to make them so. As a race we have agreed on a viewpoint and stuck by it, teaching our children that 'this is what is' and 'that is what isn't'. In so doing we have merely reinforced the accepted version of reality. As Sheldrake might say we have decided not to change the M field associated with reality perception.

Yet, sometimes children grow without such indoctrination and they in turn find themselves living in a universe that differs from the one accepted by their peers. If they can cope with the enormous pressures and isolation this must bring, they mature into adults who *see* things, *hear* things, *feel* things and *do* things that are alien to the rest of us.

Inevitably these riders on the edge of perception need to come up with their own explanations for the experiences that occur. Science guffaws in its haughty way, saying 'we are concerned with investigating reality not your fantasies'. Their unawakened family and friends may smile indulgently and say 'Well, it isn't really their fault, is it?' The media, playing a game that seems to entertain most of us, use these folk as weapons in a ratings war, beating rival sources across the head and sensationalizing and trivializing an inherent and exciting truth about our lives.

It is barely surprising that these victims often evade all responsibility for their encounter and say: 'That image and the message that I had; it did not come from me . . . a spirit person gave it to me' (quoth the medium); 'that missing time that was swallowed from my life when I spotted a peculiar light above the road, it was something external . . . the UFOnauts did it' —

so say many in this age of outer space.

We do not yet know if they are right to pass the buck and abrogate complete responsibility. But they are certainly the medium through which the message passes.

It may be that these monsters are spreading and increasing in number for esoteric reasons. If there is a planetary M field then it can hardly be unaffected by what is happening in our wonderful, 'enlightened' age. We are murdering whole species with their own M fields in the name of progress or sport. Whilst our M field may perhaps be the one that contributes most to the planet, it is foolhardy to ignore the importance of others. This is a balanced universe and an ecological planet: that ecology is being pushed over a cliff by our stupidity.

We dump sewage in our rivers and seas because it is cheap to do so. We debate whether we should do something about gaping holes in the ozone layer, letting dangerous radiation pour in from space. We exist in a selfish, offensive manner and this simply must have an effect on the planetary M field.

However, I think there is a more simple reason why monsters are on the rampage. Communication has become *the* thing in the second half of this century. Through radio, TV, satellite TV, newspapers, magazines — nothing of any significance (or more often what is *perceived* as significance) happens in the world without instant transmission. The facts, or more probably the most commercialized and exciting version of the facts, quickly gets around.

A thousand years ago window areas were known to just a few who resided in the locality, and the stories about them were handed down by word of mouth. They grew, prospered, altered and were moulded slowly into legends.

A hundred years ago the world was very different. In a week or so one could pass on news like this and a few people began to see patterns in the data. We did not yet have the science to encompass them, and we only knew a fraction of what was going on. But these tales were perceived as interesting and the creed of the supernatural was constructed as scaffolding, propping them up until we could do something with them.

Nowadays, a window becomes active and someone sensitive is there at the time. What happens? Instantly the reporters and the TV cameras arrive and the paranormal investigators investigate. Tabloid tales, TV dramas, blockbuster books all appear. Nobody remains unaware. Nobody is immune. We are changing the M field all the time by constantly writing about it, thinking about it and knowing when others are encountering it.

I think we can see what this means. Some window areas (small ones, frequently inactive, or just not recognized) will produce the occasional tale which seems isolated. Others (larger, often active and celebrated by local, or even global, legend) will become the abode of our most infamous monsters.

I suggest that the physical effects at these places are real. There may be radiation or electric fields that can tingle, prickle, hum and buzz, ionize car engines or radio sets and induce burns or nausea. Visually the phenomena are real as well: the gases, vapours, clouds and emissions that result from the natural processes, or the ionized glows — the 'earthlights' — that some researchers think these areas occasionally generate.

Let us pause and look at a couple of cases that came my way as I was writing this concluding chapter. They are typical of what is flowing in all the time and we can now look at them with a new insight.

Denise Alexander,* a young woman from Bury, Lancashire, wrote to me to describe an event that occurred on (we think) 11 February 1988. The date is important, because it is just 24 hours before a woman very nearby had an 'alien abduction' after watching Dynasty on TV and amidst a period when strange lights were flitting about the English countryside. Clearly some factor was making window areas active during this period and research could tell us what that factor was. Perhaps it was geological, or meteorological, or physical. Science could find out if it woke up from its repudiation and denials and started to pose the question in the first place.

Denise was travelling to work on the road between Bacup and Todmorden, straddling the Lancashire/West Yorkshire border. We already know about the things going on in this local window, within the highly active region of many windows (the Pennine Hills). We have had UFOs in quarries, alien big cats roaming the Bacup hills and a policeman abducted from his patrol car at Todmorden, to name just a few of the incidents in this small geographical area.

At 8.10 p.m. Denise was on the A681 at Sharneyford, close

to the county border. Within a mile either side of here I have myself seen some slightly unusual lights above a pond at Weir and a truck driver at Heald Moor had a terrifying meeting with glowing figures by the roadside.

Looking south over the hill Denise was gazing towards a reservoir. It was in this area that she saw 'a brilliant orange light . . . like a sodium streetlight, but brighter. I would say it was about one-third to one-quarter the size of the full moon. It appeared to be roughly egg-shaped, stood on end and seemed to swirl. The whole thing was like a swirling liquid (or fire embers) with constantly changing patterns. I don't think this was an illusion because I've looked at distant lights since but have not been able to get the same effect.'

Lest you think this *was* just a fire on the hillside, ponder this. Denise watched it for two or three minutes as it hovered. The slopes below were silhouetted. She could clearly perceive that it was in the sky, about 100 feet above the hill. After wondering what it was Denise decided to leave, but the object seemed to grow dimmer. She stopped the car again and now it was much duller and moving away to the south west. It appeared to gather speed as if rushing to ground and vanished in seconds either into the hill or behind it. The car window was down all the time. There was total silence on this desolate moorland road.

I was impressed by Denise. There was nothing special about her. She tried to explain the thing, likening it (without persuading herself) to a helicopter with a searchlight she had seen once. She had also observed it impeccably, measuring its motion against fenceposts beside the road.

Her account and sketch of the swirling orange egg seems to be a perfect description of the sort of light effect — the blob — which sometimes manifests around these windows. It was completely real, totally physical. It may well have been trackable on radar. It certainly could have been photographed. Indeed, we have some excellent photographs of the same type of blob taken at other window areas, notably Hessdalen in Norway.

Denise Alexander, like most witnesses, just happened to be there at the right moment. Nothing more. Had she been 'psychic' (or an fpp), then the outcome would have been quite different.

A second case was first reported to me by Barry Heathfield,

editor of the *Staffordshire Newsletter*. He had received a story from two witnesses and asked for my comments. I pointed out that the location, Cannock Chase, an area of broad heath and forest between Stafford and Birmingham, had generated a lot of reports of strange phenomena. Indeed I called it a 'notorious spot for sightings' and promised that an investigation would be launched, not least because physical traces were allegedly left in the wake of this one.

I contacted Clive Potter, who is regional investigations co-ordinator for the area. Along with Kevin Flannery and Susan Dean he set an immediate enquiry into motion.

Reg Morgan, a power station engineer, had been with his friend, Gloria Hall, to a Gingerbread meeting in Cannock on the evening of 3 August 1988. Mr Morgan had recently become a widower, although still young, and the idea of the meetings was to bring single parents together for mutual support.

They were returning to a village near Stafford shortly after midnight as 4 August began. As they approached a bridge not far from Little Hayward Mrs Hall saw a glow ahead of them. Shortly afterwards, as Mr Morgan turned the car to the right, he looked in front and saw it also. Mrs Hall had been watching for deer, not uncommon in the area late at night, and at first she instinctively warned Reg, thinking it was something that he might collide with.

Gloria Hall describes it as 'a big cloud on the floor — all red — and it lit up'. She later added that it was fluorescent and slowly pulsated (or rather the central glow was being 'eclipsed' by vapour). It seemed denser in the middle, with vaporous mist on the edges. They could not determine if there was any solid shape behind.

Reg Morgan confirmed: 'It was like a gas cloud . . . like a semi-saucer shape — a red glow — like if you look through a fluorescent tube.' When he first saw it the cloud was airborne and spanning the road. It moved away from them to the north, faded out, crossed the River Trent by the bridge and then briefly reappeared on the far side, before vanishing. The glow was certainly self-luminous. Reconstruction at the site proved there was no ambient light and the car headlamps could not have illuminated the thing.

There were no smells detected or apparent after effects. But during the sighting a clear indication of the Oz factor was mentioned.

Gloria spontaneously remarked: 'It was dead quiet . . . very, very quiet.' Roger later confirmed: 'It was unbelievably quiet' and Gloria emphasized: 'There was silence about everywhere.'

One witness in a similar case from North Yorkshire put it in a way that has always stuck in my mind: 'Nothing was doing nothing.'

Furthermore, Gloria was clearly the more affected of the two. She saw it first, remember, something Reg seemed slightly puzzled by, saying at one point: 'I don't know why it was blanked out to me.' Possibly important in that regard, Gloria noted: 'I felt weird' and tried to describe a vague unease or alteration in her state of consciousness.

Upon return they reported it immediately to the police, who took details and said that someone would come to see them. Nobody ever did. A friend of theirs reported it to the paper. They had not planned this, but were quite willing to tell a reporter what happened and be photographed at the site.

On the spot, next day, they found damage to the hedge. The blob had been first seen behind this hedge, which it had obscured when it rose from the ground, also obscuring a road warning sign. The bark on the branches was stripped and looked as if a force had crushed it. And the leaves were dehydrated.

After the story appeared in the paper Reg and Gloria noted one curious anecdote. A few days after the feature they passed the spot, as they do regularly. An unmarked white Land Rover was parked there (in the middle of nowhere) and two men wearing overalls were apparently examining the ground. Perhaps this is just coincidence, or perhaps some official organization *did* take more interest in the case than it appeared to do.

The investigation of this case was first class. Everything that could have been done was done, although (not surprisingly) there was a concentration on the physics of the event.

A whole host of significant information emerged.

Dr Michele Clare, whom we met earlier, is by profession a plant biologist. She studied soil, bark and leaf samples (and some nearby unaffected control samples). Nothing unusual was found, but it was possible to demonstrate from the presence of micro-organisms that no substantial heating was involved. This makes sense, because the witnesses felt no heat despite their close proximity to the cloud, so whatever caused the red glow was not a rise in temperature.

Dr Terence Meaden, editor of the *Journal of Meteorology*, also assisted the case study. Weather records show that the conditions involved a good deal of dewy drizzle, although a clearing weather system was sweeping through. The close proximity to the River Trent should also be noted.

David Reynolds, a local meteorologist, visited the site with investigators for a more detailed analysis. He found some evidence of tree damage which suggested a rotating vortex could have passed by. The general opinion of the weathermen involved seemed to be that the mechanical damage noted afterwards (if it was directly linked with the glowing cloud) was created by a vortex associated with the blob. The glow itself was probably ionization. Certainly there was no physical evidence on the ground that any heavy, dense or metallic object had landed and taken off again.

We may notice another point from Persinger's work. The red colour, just as theory predicts, probably occurred because of the saturation of water vapour in the atmosphere at the site. If it had been completely dry, or further from the river, the colour would have probably been blue or white.

Geologically, the area is on a boundary between sandstone and shale rocks. Quartz is certainly present. Three fault lines lie within less than a mile of the precise location.

Again there have been reports of other luminous effects in the area in the past. Paul Devereux claimed Staffordshire as a primary hot spot in his initial 'earthlights' research. Janet and Colin Bord list a number of incidents in the region in their survey of *Modern Mysteries of Britain*. My own records have many others. These include a small entity with a large domed head seen in a field at Brocton, just over a mile away, and a voice speaking into the mind of a witness at Oulton, apparently emerging from a column of light coming out of the ground.

To cap it all, less than a mile from the site is a place called Hell Hole, which seems to indicate that strange events in the area may well date back into the past.

The local newspaper story was headed 'Glowing UFO shock

for pair' and the editor phoned me for a quote on behalf of the British UFO Research Association. But the witnesses never said it was a UFO. In fact they reported it very carefully and accurately. We impose the UFO context onto this blob.

It seems that neither witness had undergone any prior psychic experiences, although that is less clear in Gloria's case. I suspect that they had a very close encounter with an ionized gas cloud emerging from the local transient; that they almost entered monster reality, given the first flutterings of the Oz factor reported, especially by Gloria; but that — possibly because they were not quite the right kind of witnesses, or maybe because they arrived as the physical component of the transient was already dissipating — the incident stopped at this early phase.

We might call this an experience of 'level one monster reality'. I suspect that in most other cases it goes no further than level one because the right combination of circumstances — i.e. the right people in the right place at just the right time — will inevitably happen only very rarely.

If they had come together in this case, and a full-blown altered state of consciousness had occurred, then who knows what the result would have been. Possibly the cloud would have 'become' a monster. Given the cultural situation it is more likely that the UFO angle would have developed. We might even have had a new time-lapse, hypnotic regression and 'memory' of an abduction by alien beings to add to our list. I think it very likely that this embryonic close encounter is exactly how these strange events begin.

If that was a level-one case, what constitutes 'level two monster reality'? Perhaps this example from Don Worley in the USA.

Rachel Baker* 'discovered she was different from other children', as she puts it, when five years old. She began to have regular premonitions. She found that if she picked up a rock from a house, images would flood into her mind and these would relate to deceased people who used to live in the building. These experiences were linked to a fall from a horse; Rachel had suffered head injuries and we must wonder if this provoked an awakening of cerebellum activity.

She married, was widowed very young, and struggled to bring up three children alone. Then on 8 December 1967 an orange glow followed her car along Duck Run Road, near her Indiana home. As her state of consciousness altered and she entered monster reality, something in her subconsious told her to turn off her normal route and onto a quiet back road.

She says: 'Suddenly the car felt like it was hit or grabbed by something . . . It was like I was being electrocuted, with stinging all over . . . I heard a humming sound, and there was an odour as if someone was gassing me . . . My head and neck were in a vice . . . It felt as if I were going down a tunnel, spinning. I had no feeling of being on the road . . . I thought I must be having some kind of strange seizure and I got ready for death.'

As you can see, by far the best way of interpreting this nightmare episode is to suggest that Rachel was the right kind of person to be sensitive to an open window (an fpp perhaps, given what we know about her). She encounters a glowing orange ball like so many other people before her, but got much closer to it. Either by accident, or other factors (an intelligence *using* her, something in her mind that acted like a magnet?) she became totally immersed within the electric field created by the active transient. Her state of consciousness turned into something akin to an epileptic attack, with the reported effects and loss of consciousness.

Rachel recovered an unknown time later. Had she been unconscious? Did she suffer a 'time lapse'? Is there any difference? She was several miles away from the location where she remembers being hit by the electric force.

Reaching home she was violently ill, had pains in her head, neck and spine and was covered in a red rash and blisters. Her body was so swollen that she could not wear a bra and her eyes were puffed out. All of this suggests that in the proximity of the transient she was exposed to radiation — possibly from microwaves. Her car radio was destroyed and the battery had been drained. So the effects of the field were very strong and localized. Clearly she was most unfortunate and simply got too close.

In the days and weeks that followed Rachel had many strange dreams. She describes seeing terrible scenes of death and destruction around the world and a feeling of being 'protected', after having been chosen as 'special' by the force behind the orange blob. She saw strange figures of various kinds during these powerful visions, mostly a four-foot tall entity with pointed chin and deep, piercing eyes.

Some of the dreams were so realistic and occurred *within* Rachel's bedroom. She reports awaking with a feeling of paralysis and dizziness and finding the ugly little creature standing next to her. There were reports of her dog being frightened and avoiding certain rooms and a smell 'like rotten eggs' prior to the appearance of the little man. She went on to have complex dreams in which she saw laboratories, human beings being cut up for food and an assembly line where the creatures 'built' people.

I think we can interpret some of these later experiences as products of her mind fantasizing around the initial 'real' encounters and inventing details to fill the puzzling gaps. That she needed to explain what had happened to her may be evidenced by the religious interpretation she placed upon the experiences.

The physically real features all tie in with what we have learnt about monster reality. Rachel is susceptible. She lives near a transient. And on several occasions she has had close encounters with the forces that emerge from this, switching into a waking lucid dream state where she may have seen the emissions of the window. The smells suggest malleable gases might have been present and there were evidently orange glows and blobs, which might have been open to 'transformation' into these ugly little men.

As Rachel was the only witness we have no need to assume that the little figures had any quasi-reality. She *could* have found herself in such a state of consciousness that she *moulded* the blobs or gases attracted to her by tinkering with their subatomic structure. Or she may have merely 'perceived' the amorphous and ambiguous shapes as ugly creatures.

Whatever the case, the result was powerful enough to convince Rachel completely. Physical effects on her body resulted, either from the real energy, or from her mind being so convinced by the realism of the encounter.[147]

The entities had a form that fits perfectly with the typical American stereotype of an 'alien entity' (the four-foot tall ugly thing with pointed chin). This appears to be the form currently adopted by the relevant M field and Rachel presumably just tuned in. Her experience had a few individual touches, but basically it followed the pre-existing template because that is exactly what morphic resonance says should happen.

Incidentally, it is worth noting that the stereotype American entity is different from that found elsewhere. South American witnesses, for example, tend to see hairy dwarfs. British witnesses often encounter tall, blond-haired humanoids. Does this suggest that there are *regional* M fields? Was Rachel attuned to the American version, whereas had she lived in Britain the resultant entity would have been more in keeping with the Anglo-Saxon M field?[148]

This is one of many questions only further research will answer.

You may wonder why we are even discussing whether Rachel Baker might have been able to sculpt her monsters from the gases or blobs that are generated by the transient. Surely this bizarre extension of the concept of monster reality is quite unnecessary? On Cannock Chase two people saw the vaporous form because it was actually there to *be* seen. In Rachel's case, we can accept that the forms reported could have just been visualized behind the glow — like the old adage about 'fairies in a fire', especially as the woman *was* in an altered state of consciousness.

However, if this theory is to work it has to account for multiple-witness experiences — situations where other people share in the monster reality. They are rare, but they do happen.

Then, of course, we have the photographic cases, like Doc Shiels' 'Nessie' images. These certainly cannot be explained as hallucinations. The monsters could be real, or every unexplained picture a fake, but the evidence makes neither of these options attractive. So only one alternative is left: 'level three monster reality' would occur when the monster *becomes* sufficiently 'real' to be visible to others.

This seems an extremely rare occurrence, which is why we have so few examples. Presumably the circumstances have to be absolutely right, with someone who is exceptionally gifted at creative visualization and probably able to perform PK in a specific kind of monster reality. And, of course, the gases or blobs have to *be* there to be adaptable.

I think it very unlikely that anything very solid or substantial can be turned into a monster. PK of that sort requires proof that we do not seem to have. In the last chapter I proposed that in such exceptional circumstances what happens is the gas, or energy blob, or dust particles are shaped by an electrical field. It is this *field* which the mind will control. But we do not see it, of course, because it is invisible. We only see a monster forming when the substance trapped by the field becomes visible.

If this idea has any validity we ought to be able to make some predictions. For one thing, many of these sculpted mind monsters would be vague and amorphous, by the nature of the substances from which they are made. Even the best would probably have something insubstantial about them. Also, because they seem to rely on shaping electrical fields, then the presence of buzzing sensations, tinglings and other hints of the presence of this energy should be found in the data.

I believe the photographic evidence does support this. The forms are often vague blobs — and we saw in the case of the American bigfoot photo that whilst the monster was witnessed by several people, it had no physical substance (bullets, for instance, went through it). Also the photograph that was taken showed nothing more than a glowing blob.

Another excellent case of what seems to be 'level three monster reality' is regarded by many as the best photograph ever taken of a UFO.

On 16 January 1958 a converted Brazilian navy vessel, the *Almirante Saldanha* was moored off an uninhabited island hundreds of miles out into the Atlantic. It was taking part in the coordinated series of global scientific experiments, the International Geophysical Year. Aboard was a naval crew and several scientists. They were setting up a weather station on this barren lump of rock.

At 12.15 p.m. in broad daylight the official ship's photographer and 47 crew members on deck at the time saw an object approach from the sea, circle round them and fly off back out to sea. Four excellent black and white shots were taken as the thing was visible. The captain — mindful of his duty as a naval officer — ordered that they be processed immediately. When he saw that they had captured the object, he ensured that as soon as the ship reached port the film and negatives were handed over to the government and, when they were satisfied that no trickery was involved, the President was to be informed.

The photographs depict a Saturn-shaped object, which matches what was visually reported. However, if we study the images in detail we see that they are extremely fuzzy and look almost like gas. Blotches of light and dark grey appear unevenly across the surface. Certainly the solidity of this 'UFO' is only superficial. Once looked at carefully we see that this was a highly vaporous form.

The eye-witnesses attest to this fuzziness. It was a real part of the sighting. They referred to a greenish 'haze' that surrounded the thing which is similar to particles of dust clinging on by electrostatic force. Also at the time of the sighting an electric winch was in operation hauling a small boat onto deck. When the thing flew by this briefly stopped working, again suggesting a local electrical field was passing over.

All the evidence points to a genuine case and the photographs

This photograph is one of a series taken by the cameraman working on a naval survey vessel moored off the uninhabited Atlantic island of Trindade during the 1957-8 'International Geophysical Year'. It shows a fuzzy blob also seen by many eye witnesses. The thing floated across the sea, inducing ionized fields into the atmosphere. This is believed to be one of the most important cases on record and is dramatic proof of 'Mind Monsters'.

being real. But they fit in perfectly with monster reality. The UFO-like image may have been sculpted by one of the percipients. In essence it was just a mass of dust, or vapour, trapped within an electrical field.[149]

Monsters are many things to many people. The information that creates them may come from outside, it may be flowing from a distant galaxy, or a planetary M field; or it may be something lurking inside us. But wherever it emerges, and whatever it is, one thing is certain: monsters are brought to our awareness by the minds of sensitive people who find themselves passing through an active window area at the appropriate moment.

The result may be imaginary, or real, or even quasi-real and forged like sculptures out of the most appropriate current version of the M field, using only the raw materials at hand.

But our monsters are mind monsters, and the mind most responsible is our own.

References

Chapter 1

1 *Miracle Visitors*, Watson, I., Gollancz, 1978; Grafton, 1980
2 'Anatomy of a percipient', Watson, N., *Magonia* 11, 12, 1978
  'Protected by angels?' Randles, J., *Northern UFO News* 97,
  1982
3 *Earth 1*, 1985
4 *Lifetide*, Watson, Dr L., Hodder and Stoughton, 1979
5 *The Unknown*, Bord, J. & C., June 1986
6 *Strange Creatures from Time and Space*, Keel, J., Spearman,
  1975
7 *BUFORA Bulletin*, September/October 1975
8 *The Unknown*, Goss, M., November 1985
9 'On monsters', Heuvelmans, B., *Fortean Times* 41, 1983
10 *Janus*, Koestler, A., Hutchinson, 1978
11 *The Magic Zoo*, Costello, P., Sphere, 1979
12 *Toward a Psychology of Being*, Maslow, A., Van Nostrand,
  1962
13 *The Radiant Child*, Armstrong, Dr T., Quest Books, 1985
14 *The Decline and Fall of Science*, Green, C., Hamish Hamilton,
  1976
15 *A Pictorial History of Science Fiction*, Kyle, D., Tiger, 1986
16 *Northern UFO News* 110, 1984
17 *Northern UFO News* 127, 1987
18 Information contained in reports from UFORA via Godic,
  V. & P.
19 *Northern UFO News* 132, 1988

Chapter 2

20 *The Magic Zoo*, op. cit., p. 158

21 *US Sun*, 17 July 1984

22 *The Unknown*, Bord, J. & C., October 1985

23 *The Unknown*, Davis, R., January 1986

24 *Fortean Times* 43, 1985

25 *STRANGE*, Box 2246, Rockville MD 20852, USA

26 *UFO Universe*, September 1988

27 *Photographs of the Unknown*, Rickard, R. & Kelly, R., NEL, 1980

28 *The Unknown*, Shuker, K., September/October 1986

29 *Nature*, Report by Fricke, H., September 1987

30 'Australia's lizard monsters', Gilroy, R., *Fortean Times* 37, 1982

31 *The Loch Ness Monster: The Evidence*, Campbell, S., Aquarian Press, 1986

32 *The Unknown*, Hough, P., August 1985

33 'Comments', Shiels, A., *Fortean Times* 23, 1977

34 *Fortean Times* 24, 1978

35 *The Unknown*, Westwood, P., March 1987

36 'Report', Rickard, R., *Fortean Times* 46, 1986

37 'Operation Deepscan', Dash, M., *Fortean Times* 50, 1988

38 'In search of dinosaurs', Mackal, Prof. R., *Fortean Times* 34, 1981

39 'The search for the evidence of the *mokele-mbembe*', Mackal, Prof. R., Greenwell, J.R., Wilkinson, M.J., *Cryptozoology* 1, 1982

40 '*Mokele-mbembe*', Regusters, Prof. H., *African Library Notes*, California Institute of Technology, July 1982

41 Letter to Bill Gibbons, dated 15 July 1985

42 Letter to me, dated 23 September 1985

43 *Fortean Times* 47, 1986

44 *Fortean Times* 46, 1986

Chapter 3

45 'Brief details' in *Flying Saucer Occupants*, Lorenzen, C. & L., Signet, 1967

46 'Encounter with "devils"', Mesnard J. & Pavy, C. (Translation by Hugill, J.), *FSR* Vol. 14, No. 5, 1968

47 *Northern UFO News* 82, 1981

48 'Bipedal humanoids in Nebraska', *Journal of the Fortean Research Center*, April 1987

49 *The Guardian*, 10 January 1987

50 *BBC Wildlife Magazine*, September 1986, pp 422–426

51 *Fortean Times* 48, 1987

52 Available via Amazing Horizons Inc., Box 61662, Sunnyvale CA 94088, USA

53 *The Unidentified*, Clark, J. & Coleman, L., Warner, 1975, pp. 14–19

54 *Abduction*, Randles, J., Robert Hale, 1988; *Headline*, 1989; *Inner Light*, 1989

55 'UFOs and the para-ape connection', Worley, D., *UFO Universe*, January 1989

56 *Alien Animals*, Bord, J. & C., Grafton, 1980, pp. 44–53

57 *The Interrupted Journey*, Fuller, J., Putnam, 1966; new edition Souvenir, 1980; Corgi, 1981; filmed as *The UFO Incident*

58 *Cat Country*, Francis, D., Exeter, 1983

59 For a summary of the Exmoor 'beast' hunt see *Fortean Times* 40, 1983

60 *Cat Flaps*, Roberts, A., Brigantia Books, 1986 (for address see *UFO Brigantia*)

61 *The Pennine UFO Mystery*, Randles, J., Grafton, 1983

62 *Sky Crash*, Butler, B., Randles, J. & Street, D., Spearman, 1984; new edition Grafton, 1986

63 'Blythburgh and Sizewell UFOs', Johnson, P., *FSR* Vol. 21, No. 5, 1976

64 *Fortean Times* 31, 1980

65 'Phantoms in suburbia', Schaffner, R., *FATE* 422, 1985

66 'The Queensland tiger', Goss, M., *FATE* 444, 1987

67 'The Livingston Case, Special Report', Campbell, S., *BUFORA*, 1982

68 *The Unknown*, Shuker, K., May 1987

69 *The Unknown*, Goss, M., November 1986

Chapter 4

70 *Scientific Study of UFOs*, Condon, Dr E. (Ed.) Bantam, 1969

71 *Light Years*, Kinder, G., Atlantic Monthly Press, 1987; Penguin, 1988

72 *Northern UFO News* 107, 1984

73 'Witnesses of UFOs and other anomalies', Weston, Dr R., *UFO Phenomena and the Behavioural Scientist*, Haines, Dr R. (Ed.), Scarecrow, 1979

74 Case report by Watson, N.

75 'The entity of death', *Death by Supernatural Causes?*, Randles, J. & Hough, P., Grafton, 1988; Bzztoh, 1989

76 'New Zealand entity reports', Basterfield, K., *UFORAN* Vol. 4, No. 2, 1983

77 *Northern UFO News* 134, 1988

78 *Abduction*, op. cit.

79 *Intruders*, Hopkins, B., Random House, 1987; Sphere, 1988

80 *Alien Contact*, Randles, J., Spearman, 1981; Coronet, 1983

81 'The abduction of Sammy Desmond', Scott Rogo, D., *International UFO Reporter*, July/August 1987

82 *UFO Reality*, Randles, J., Robert Hale, 1983
'Fire in the sky', Randles, J., *BUFORA*, 1989

83 Randles, J. & Grimshawe, T., *FSR* Vol. 23, No. 2, 1977

84 Cox, T., *FSR* Vol. 24, No. 1, 1978

85 *Northern UFO News* 120, 1986

86 *Northern UFO News* 112, 1985

87 *The Janos People*, Johnson, F., Spearman, 1980

Chapter 5

88 *Modern Mysteries of Britain*, Bord J. & C., Grafton, 1987

89 *Sixth Sense*, Randles, J., Robert Hale, 1987

90 'Folklore, myths and legends of Britain', Ross, Dr A., *Readers Digest*, 1973

91 *Circles of Silence*, Robins, Dr D., Souvenir, 1985

92 *Communion*, Strieber, W., Century Hutchinson, 1987; Arrow, 1988
Transformation, Strieber, W., Century Hutchinson, 1988; Arrow, 1989

93 'UFO abductions and the Celtic otherworld', Clarke, D., *UFO Brigantia* November/December 1988

94 *Alien Contact*, op. cit.

95 'Fake photos, real sightings', Randles, J., *International UFO Reporter* November/December 1986

96 *Northern UFO News* 117, 1986

97 *UFOs: A British Viewpoint*, Randles, J. & Warrington, P., Robert Hale, 1979, pp. 143–5

98 *UFO Study*, Randles, J., Robert Hale, 1981, pp. 167–71

99 Musgrave, J.B., *FSR* Vol. 23, No. 2, 1977

100 *Northern UFO News* 118, 1986

101 Earp, F., in *Northern Earth Mysteries*, February 1981

102 *Alien Contact*, op. cit.

103 *Understanding Epilepsy*, Burden, G. & Schurr, P., Grafton, 1980

104 *Fairy Tales*, Cooper, J.C., Aquarian Press, 1983

105 *The Secret Commonwealth of Elves, Fauns and Fairies*, Kirk, R., Sterling, 1933

106 *Readers Digest*, op. cit.

Chapter 6

107 Clarke, D., Oldroyd, G. & Watson, N., published by FUFOR, Box 277, Mount Rainier, MD 20712, USA

108 'Psychic parallelism in the "Green Stone" affair', Randles, J., *Common Ground* 10, 1986

Chapter 7

109 *A summary of studies on luminous phenomena accompanying earthquakes*, Yasui, Y., Dokkyo Medical University, Tokyo, 1974

110 *Space-time Transients and Unusual Phenomena*, Persinger, Dr M. & Lafrenière, G., Nelson-Hall, 1977

111 'Possible infrequent geophysical sources of close UFO encounters', Persinger, Dr M., *UFO Phenomena and the Behavioural Scientist*, Haines, Dr R. (Ed.), Scarecrow, 1979

112 *When the Snakes Awake*, Tributsch, Dr H., MIT Press, 1982

113 *Earthlights*, Devereux, P. & McCartney, Dr P., Turnstone Press, 1982

114 *The Pennine UFO Mystery*, op. cit.

115 'UFOs as natural phenomena', Rutkowski, C., *UFOs: 1947–1987*, Evans, H. & Spencer, J. (Eds), BUFORA/Fortean Times, 1987

116 'Earthlights', Devereux, P., *Phenomenon*, Evans, H. & Spencer, J. (Eds), Macdonald Futura, 1988; Avon, 1989

117 'Possible increased cancer and depression risk among UFO field researchers and populations near "flap" areas', Persinger, Dr M., *MUFON Journal*, August 1988

118 *The Earthlights Revelation*, Devereux, P. et al., Cassell, 1989

119 *Phantoms of the Skies*, Clarke, D. & Roberts, A., Robert Hale, 1990

120 *Magonia*, Watson, N., op. cit.

121 *Sunset of the Mind*, Kenworthy, C., unpublished, 1989

122 *Flying Saucers: A Modern Myth of Things Seen in the Skies*, Jung, Dr C. Routledge and Kegan Paul, 1959

123 *The UFO Evidence*, Hall, R. (Ed), NICAP, 1964

124 'Folklore scholarship and UFO reality', Bullard, Dr T., *International UFO Reporter* July/August 1988

125 *Mindsplit*, McKellar, Prof. P., Dent, 1979

126 'The fantasy-prone personality: Implications for understanding images, hypnosis and parapsychological exophenomena', Wilson, S. & Barber, T., *Imagery*, Shekh, A. (Ed.), John Wiley, 1983

127 'Distal eidetic technology: Further considerations of the fantasy-prone personality', Myers, S. & Austrin, H., *Journal of Mental Imagery* Vol. 9, No. 3, 1985

128 'The fantasy-prone person: hypnosis, imagination and creativity', Lynn, S. & Rhue, J., *Journal of Personality* Vol. 51, No. 2, 1986
'Fantasy proneness: developmental antecedents', Lynn, S. & Rhue, J., *Journal of Personality* Vol. 55, No. 1, 1987

129 *UFOs: The Image Hypothesis*, Basterfield, K., Reed, 1981

130 *Flying Saucer Abductees and Contactees: Psychopathology or Fantasy-prone?* Bartholomew, Dr R. & Basterfield, K., unpublished, 1988

131 'Abductions: the fantasy-prone personality hypothesis', Bartholomew, Dr R. & Basterfield, K., *International UFO Reporter* May/June 1988

132 *Intruders*, op. cit.

133 *International UFO Reporter* July/August 1985; July/August 1987

134 *Abduction*, op. cit.

135 Letters published by *International UFO Reporter* July/August 1988

136 *The Natural History of the Mind*, Rattray-Taylor, G., Secker & Warburg, 1979; Grafton, 1981

137 *The Secret Life of Humans*, Gooch, Dr S., Dent, 1981

138 *The Double Helix of the Mind*, Gooch, Dr S., Wildwood House, 1980

139 *Lucid Dreams*, Green, C., Oxford Institute of Psycho-physical Research, 1968

140 *The Dancing Wu Li Masters*, Zukov, G., Rider Hutchinson, 1979, p. 114

141 *A New Science of Life*, Sheldrake, Dr R., Blond & Briggs, 1981; Paladin, 1983

142 New edition: Paladin, 1987

143 *Fortean Times* 37, 1982

144 See discussion in *Sixth Sense*, op. cit., pp. 168–170

145 Sheldrake, Dr R., in *New Scientist*, 11 February 1988

146 *A New Science of Life*, op. cit., p. 103

Conclusions

147 'Rachel Baker and her little friends', Worley, D., *Official UFO*, February 1976

148 *Abduction*, op. cit.

149 Smith, Dr W. in *International UFO Reporter* July/August 1983

Addresses

BUFORA 16 South Way, Burgess Hill, Sussex RH15 9ST
FATE PO Box 64383, St Paul, MN 55164–0383, USA
FORTEAN TIMES 1 Shoebury Road, London E6 2AQ
FSR Snodland, Maidstone, Kent ME6 5HJ
INTERNATIONAL UFO REPORTER 2457 W. Peterson, Chicago, IL 60659, USA
JOURNAL OF FORTEAN RESEARCH CENTER PO Box 94627, Lincoln, NE 68509, USA
MAGONIA 5 James Terrace, London SW14 8HB
MUFON JOURNAL 103 Oldtowne Road, Seguin, TX 78155, USA
NORTHERN EARTH MYSTERIES 6 Old Retford Road, Handsworth, Sheffield S13 9QZ
NORTHERN UFO NEWS 37 Heathbank Road, Cheadle Heath, Stockport, Cheshire SK3 0UP
UFO BRIGANTIA 84 Elland Road, Brighouse, West Yorkshire HD6 2QR
UFO CALL (Updated news reports from BUFORA and British Telecom, presented by Jenny Randles) Phone (0898) 121886 (Britain only)
UFO RESEARCH AUSTRALIA PO Box 229, Prospect, South Australia 5082
UFO UNIVERSE 351 West 54th Street, New York, NY 10019, USA

Index